CONTRACTUAL CORRESPONDENCE
FOR ARCHITECTS
AND PROJECT MANAGERS

Third Edition

David Chappell
BA (Hons Arch), MA (Arch), MA (Law), PhD, RIBA
Architect and Contracts Consultant
Chappell-Marshall Limited

Blackwell
Science

© David Chappell 1983, 1989, 1996

Blackwell Science Ltd
Editorial Offices:
Osney Mead, Oxford OX2 0EL
25 John Street, London WC1N 2BL
23 Ainslie Place, Edinburgh EH3 6AJ
238 Main Street, Cambridge,
    Massachusetts 02142, USA
54 University Street, Carlton,
    Victoria 3053, Australia

Other Editorial Offices:
Arnette Blackwell SA
    224, Boulevard Saint Germain
    75007 Paris
    France

Blackwell Wissenschafts-Verlag GmbH
    Kurfürstendamm 57
    10707 Berlin, Germany

Zehetnergasse 6
A-1140 Wien
Austria

First edition published 1983
    by The Architectural Press Ltd
Second edition published 1989
    by Legal Studies & Services Ltd
Third edition published 1996
    by Blackwell Science Ltd

Set in 10.5pt Times
by DP Photosetting, Aylesbury, Bucks
Printed and bound in Great Britain by
Hartnolls Ltd, Bodmin, Cornwall

DISTRIBUTORS

Marston Book Services Ltd
PO Box 87
Oxford OX2 0DT
(*Orders:* Tel: 01865 791155
        Fax: 01865 791927
        Telex: 837515)

USA
Blackwell Science, Inc.
238 Main Street
Cambridge, MA 02142
(*Orders:* Tel: 800 215-1000
        617 876-7000
        Fax: 617 492-5263)

Canada
Copp Clarke, Ltd
2775 Matheson Blvd East
Mississauga, Ontario
Canada, L4W 4P7
(*Orders:* Tel: 800 263-4374
        905 238-6074)

Australia
Blackwell Science Pty Ltd
54 University Street
Carlton, Victoria 3053
(*Orders:* Tel: 03 9347-0300
        Fax: 03 9349 3016)

A catalogue record for this book is
available from the British Library

ISBN 0–632–04002–5

Library of Congress
Cataloging-in-Publication Data
Chappell, David.
    Contractual correspondence for
architects/David Chappell.—3rd ed.
        p. cm.
    Includes index.
    ISBN 0–632–04002–5
    1. Architectural contracts—Great
Britain—Forms. 2. Architects—
Legal status, laws, etc.—Great Britain—
Forms. I. Title.
KD1641.A65C45 1996
344.41'0176172—dc20
[344.104176172]   95-47344
                                        CIP

Contents

Preface to the Third Edition

This was the first book I wrote. It was with mixed feelings, some fourteen books later, that I approached the task of revision and inserting additional material to bring it up to date. The first edition was extremely well received particularly by architects, for whom it was written. It clearly filled a need for a handy book to help solve a few common problems. The somewhat enlarged second edition enjoyed continuing success and I sincerely hope that this new version will continue to act as a lifebelt in tricky situations.

The revisions have again been extensive. There has been much case law in the seven years since the second edition and, although this is not a legal textbook and contains no references to decided cases, they have been taken into account in framing the advice and model letters. In addition, the Joint Contracts Tribunal have issued some important contract amendments which have affected many of the sections. Account has been taken of all amendments up to 15 for JCT 80, up to 9 for IFC 84 and up to 9 for MW 80.

There has been some criticism of the idea of model letters and the use of rather formal language in those letters. I remain firmly unrepentant on both issues. I have never, and do not, advocate the use of model letters without the input of some brain activity. Thus, circumstances and people demand differing approaches. Having said that, there is no doubt that model letters, sensibly used, are a tremendous aid to a busy practitioner. As for the language: wherever possible I have used the precise wording of the contract. This makes clear to the recipient that the letter is written pursuant to the appropriate clause. In other cases, I have tried to be clear, concise and precise. It is for the user to make whatever amendments may seem fit in the circumstances. Informality in contractual correspondence is rarely, if ever, warranted, but in any case my informality is not yours and it would be out of place in a book like this.

Over the years I have been fortunate in having had the benefit of comments from my friend Professor Vincent Powell-Smith. Many of the revisions in this edition are a direct result of very perceptive comments by my friend and colleague Derek Marshall, who will be surprised to read this. This is also an appropriate place to acknowledge advice from the late Raymond Cecil who read through the whole book in the first edition and gave me detailed notes in his own inimitable style. I am grateful to him for his views even though I have not adopted all of them. Caroline Dalziel, at short notice, undertook the tedious job of proof reading and preparing the index, for which I am most grateful. Finally, thanks to my wife Margaret.

David Chappell, 1996
Chappell–Marshall Limited
27 Westgate
Tadcaster
North Yorkshire
LS24 9JB

Introduction

There are many good contractual handbooks available to assist the architect to carry out his duties properly. The RIBA *Architect's Job-book*, *Legal and Contractual Procedures for Architects* by Bob Greenstreet and David Chappell, *The Architects Guide to Running a Job* by Ronald Green, and the Chartered Institute of Builders *Code of Practice for Project Management for Construction and Development* are just some of the excellent manuals available, each with its own particular approach. Contractual handbooks and procedural manuals, however, are intended to ensure that jobs proceed smoothly or, at any rate, within the prescribed limits of normal procedures. When things go wrong, the architect must turn to the legal textbooks which require time and knowledge to study.

Between the two extremes, a smooth contract or a catastrophe, there is a gap which this book attempts to fill. It is based on the fact that architects, contractors, consultants and clients will forget things, do them at the wrong time or simply make mistakes. In addition, numerous problems arise which the architect cannot foresee. Problems tend to follow a pattern. The author has personally encountered or observed most of the situations set out on the pages which follow. The intention is to help the architect extricate himself from difficulties in the most practical way.

This is not a legal textbook. The opinions expressed are those of the author who makes no claim to infallibility. Court and arbitration proceedings are fraught with uncertainty. Try not to be a test case. If in doubt you should always take sound advice.

Note:

- For ease of reference, the book follows the RIBA Plan of Work. Items are located where one would normally expect to find them.
- JCT 1980 Standard Form 'With Quantities (JCT 80)' is assumed to have been used.
- All items are applicable to the 'Without Quantities' edition. The difference, noted in the text, being chiefly that schedules of work or a specification is used instead of bills of quantities.

❏ Notes and alternatives have been given, where necessary, to show how the items are applicable when the Intermediate Form of Contract (IFC 84) or Agreement for Minor Building Works (MW 80) is used. Where there are differences, additional notes are added under the headings IFC 84 or MW 80 as appropriate. Thus if the comments under JCT 80 and IFC 84 are the same, but MW 80 required different comments, only the main text and a reference to MW 80 would be given.

❏ *The Standard Form of Agreement for the Appointment of an Architect* 1992 (SFA 92) or the *Conditions of Engagement* 1995 (CE/95) (the successor to *Architect's Appointment*) is assumed to have been used and the appropriate scales and terms of engagement agreed with the client.

❏ For convenience the masculine gender has been used throughout. 'He' may be taken to mean 'she', 'his' to mean 'hers' etc.

❏ Numbers in brackets in headings and text refer to the numbers of the relevant letters.

❏ Every letter should have a heading, clearly stating the job title. Only letter 1 has been shown in this way to avoid needless repetition.

No attempt has been made to cover the perfectly routine matters adequately covered by other manuals. See the author's *Standard Letters in Architectural Practice* for more routine matters. The presentation is a series of problems. It is hoped that the inclusion of a large number of standard letters will be helpful, not only for use as model letters to deal with specific difficulties, but in indicating the kind of letter suitable for similar although not identical situations. Each letter should be adjusted in tone to suit the recipient. The Appendices contain sections on writing letters and making decisions.

A Inception

A1 Client's bona fides: in doubt (1)

A new client often makes an appearance quite suddenly and you may know little or nothing about him. The request for your services may come in the form of a letter, telephone call or personal approach.

Bearing in mind that many problems between architect and client owe their origins to an initial misunderstanding, you must go through the normal procedure of appointment including a very clear agreement on its precise terms and the fees payable. The fact that your client is well known (and even respected) in his own profession is no guarantee that he will, or can, pay your fees.

If you are at all uncertain about your client's ability to pay your fees, there are two things you can do immediately after receiving the initial approach:

❏ Take out references
❏ Ask the client for a payment on account

Both procedures require careful consideration before putting them into operation. References usually can be obtained through your own bank on a confidential basis but your prospective client may well discover that you have been making enquiries and take offence. There are also firms who specialise in providing this kind of information. Much depends upon the type of client. In the present economic climate the taking up of references is commonplace before any sort of credit is extended. You alone will be in a position to gauge your client's probable reaction.

The alternative, which is much favoured by the legal profession, is sometimes a good way to test the serious intentions of a previously unknown client.

If you hear nothing further, your suspicions were probably well founded. If your client proceeds with the meeting, you must be sure to have a clear agreement of the sum payable on account written into your terms of appointment. The precise sum will depend upon your assessment of:

1   Letter from architect to client if bona fides in doubt

Dear Sir

<u>Proposed Office Block at Back Road, Metrotown</u>

Thank you for your letter [*amend as appropriate if the approach is by telephone or in person*] of [*insert date*] instructing me to carry out architectural services in connection with the above project.

I should be pleased to visit you/see you at this office [*delete as appropriate*] to discuss your detailed requirements and my terms of appointment. I would ask for a payment on account of [*insert percentage*] of the estimated total fees[1] at the time of signing the agreement.

A copy of the RIBA *Standard Form of Agreement for the Appointment of an Architect* is enclosed. When you have had the opportunity to peruse it, perhaps you will telephone me to arrange a convenient date and time for our meeting.

Yours faithfully

---

[1] *You may prefer to insert an actual sum rather than a percentage. It may prevent disputes.*

❑ The size of the job
❑ The client

Finally, you must be sure to get your payment before starting work.

A2 Fee recovery (2), (3), (4), (5), (Fig. 1)

A difficult problem, which should be considered at the beginning of every project, is how to collect fees. Theoretically, you will submit invoices for amounts and at intervals previously agreed and your client will pay. It seldom happens quite like that. Fees have more often to be coaxed or threatened from your client depending on circumstances. It is assumed that you have entered into a proper fee agreement before starting work. If not, you are not so much asking for trouble as laying a red carpet and begging it to come through your door.

You should make the manner and timing of payments part of your agreement. Your client may well appreciate being able to make regular payments because it will enable him to programme his own financial commitment more accurately. Once you have agreed upon a system of regular payments, send accounts regularly and insist on payment. You may find it convenient to send out all your accounts on a monthly basis. One advantage of a regular fee commitment is that you will have early warning if your client misses a payment. Remember that if your client does not pay you, he is in breach of his contract. A sign that your client may be in financial difficulties is if he suddenly begins to question your fee accounts without good reason. Learn to recognise the signs and act accordingly.

You should set up your own system of collecting fees. As a guide, you could use the following procedure, but be ready to vary it depending upon your personal knowledge of your client:

❑ Send out fee accounts as soon as you can and keep a chart of all fees billed and outstanding with notes of reminders **(Fig. 1)**
❑ Send a first reminder letter one month after the date of the fee account **(2)**
❑ Send a second reminder seven days later **(3)**
❑ After a further seven days, telephone or visit your client if the amount warrants it. At this time state that you must have your fee within seven days
❑ Seven days later send letter threatening legal action **(4)**
❑ Seven days later take legal action

If you have reason to believe that you will not be paid, you should curtail the reminders and threaten legal action at an early date. Clearly,

2   Letter from architect to client – first reminder

Dear Sir

[*insert appropriate heading*]

I refer to my fee account dated [*insert date*] in the sum of £ [*insert amount*] which is still outstanding.

In view of the current economic climate, you will appreciate that I rely upon clients to settle accounts promptly. No doubt the matter has escaped your attention, but I should be pleased if you would let me have your cheque by return of post.

Yours faithfully

3 Letter from architect to client – second reminder

Dear Sir

[*insert appropriate heading*]

I refer to my fee account dated [*insert date*] in the sum of [*insert amount*] and my letter of [*insert date*]. I regret to note that I have not yet received payment.

Would you please give this matter your immediate attention?

Yours faithfully

4 Letter from architect to client – threatening legal action

Dear Sir

[*insert appropriate heading*]

I refer to my fee account dated [*insert date*] in the sum of [*insert amount*] which has not yet been paid despite reminders.

In view of the relationship which exists between us, I have not pursued this matter with the vigour it deserves. Although I have no wish to cause difficulties for you, I must have regard to my own financial position. I regret, therefore, that if I do not receive your cheque for the full amount outstanding by first post on [*insert date seven days following date of letter*], I shall have no alternative but to instruct my solicitors to commence proceedings for recovery of the debt. I do hope that it will not become necessary.

Yours faithfully

Client	Fees billed	Date	First reminder (4 weeks)	Date	Second reminder (7 days)	Date	Telephone /visit (7 days)	Date	Threaten legal action (7 days)	Date	Take action (7 days)	Date
A Ltd	3000	20.2.96	✓	20.3.96	✓	27.3.96	T ✓	3.4.96	✓	10.4.96	(PAID)	17.4.96
B Ltd	4500	20.2.96	✓	20.3.96	(PAID)	27.3.96						
Mr C	700	20.2.96	✓	20.3.96					✓	27.3.96	Solicitor	3.4.96
D Ltd	1100	20.2.96	(PAID)	21.2.96								
E Ltd	5000	4.3.96	(PAID)	12.3.96								
F Ltd	25	20.3.96	✓	17.4.96	✓	24.4.96			✓	1.5.96	(PAID)	2.5.96
G Ltd	7000	4.4.96	✓	2.5.96	✓	9.5.96	V ✓	16.5.96	✓	23.5.96	Solicitor	30.4.96
H Ltd	200	17.4.96	(PAID)	19.4.96								
Mrs J	25000	17.4.96	✓	15.5.96	(PAID)	21.5.96						
Miss K	500	17.4.96	(PAID)	13.5.96								
L Ltd	5500	17.4.96	✓	15.5.96	(PAID)	25.5.96						

Fig. 1 Fee recovery chart.

5 Letter from architect to client 'accepting' lesser payment in full satisfaction

Dear Sir

[*insert appropriate heading*]

Thank you for your letter of [*insert date*].

I note that you agree that you owe [*insert amount*]. You have explained your difficulties and offered me the sum of [*insert amount*] in full satisfaction of my outstanding fees.

Reluctantly, I accept and I look forward to receiving your payment.

Yours faithfully

if you do take action through the courts to obtain payment, it is extremely unlikely that your client will ask you to work for him again. Splendid; if you have any sense, you will not accept such a commission even if offered. Always remember that your survival is at stake. If your client tells you, after the first reminder, that he is temporarily embarrassed financially, but that he is confident of paying you within, say, a month or six weeks or in instalments, you will have to use your judgment whether to accept his offer. If you do, get it in writing. If he fails to pay as he promises, take action. On no account agree to postpone your fees in this way twice with the same client and do not consider giving him extra time to pay if he waits until you threaten action before he tells you of his difficulties. This is merely a guide. How you react in any given set of circumstances is for you to decide. Remember that many individuals and firms make a habit of paying at the last possible moment. It makes good economic sense and they can be very plausible in formulating excuses.

In most cases you will recover fees after you have sent one or two reminders and certainly before you put your threat of legal action into effect. There will always be some instances, however, where legal action is your only hope.

If the sum outstanding is substantial, it is a good idea to speak to your solicitor before you threaten legal action. He may advise you to incorporate a rehearsal of the facts in your letter together with dates of all letters of reminder in order to form a sound base for proceedings. He may well draft the letter for you.

Your client may offer to pay a lesser sum than you demand 'in full settlement' of your fee; otherwise, he may say, you will get nothing. Do not hesitate to accept provided that:

❏ Your client has accepted that he owes you the full amount *and*
❏ There is no consideration attached to the payment of the lesser sum

Having received the lesser sum, you can if you so wish sue for the remainder. Your letter of acceptance should follow the lines of Letter **(5)**. If, however, you agree to accept a lesser sum 'in full settlement' of fees which the client is disputing, your acceptance is binding because you are both compromising the dispute and consideration is present. The handling of the matter requires great care and if you are in any doubt about it, you should consult your solicitor.

Of course, it is always better to accept a lesser sum or payment of very small sums stretching to infinity than to waste time and money chasing an insolvent client.

A3 Appointment, if architect asked to tender on fees (6)

It is now quite common to be asked to provide a lump sum fee quotation before being commissioned to carry out work. This can occur even if you are the sole architect being considered, but it may indicate that several architects are being asked to tender on fees. There is nothing basically wrong with this; it is covered by principle 3, rules 3.2 and 3.3 of the RIBA Code of Professional Conduct. The crucial points to observe are:

❑ Do not quote a fee unless your prospective client has invited you to do so
❑ Before quoting, you must have enough information to know the kind of work required, its scope and the precise services your client wants you to provide
❑ You must not fall into the trap of revising your quotation (always downwards of course) to undercut another architect who is quoting for the same service

Some architects still refuse to tender on fees as a matter of principle. Although there is no real evidence that such architects fare any the worse as a result, it is a fact of modern architectural life that most organisations now operate some kind of fee tendering arrangement. Of course, just because you tender on fees to get a job does not mean that you must cut your fees to the bone. Indeed there is every reason why you should not do that. If your quotation is so low that you are unable to provide the level of service which your client expects, you will simply lose money on the project as you fight an impossible battle between time and costs.

An essential preliminary to fee tendering is cost recording. Only by keeping careful records of what it costs you to carry out a job can you hope to produce reasonably accurate forecasts of future work. Until you have this vital information, steer clear of fee tendering or include a generous amount for contingencies.

A4 Brief: difficulty in obtaining decisions (7), (8)

Despite your best efforts, you may find that your client is very slow in giving you decisions or he may try to leave decisions to you which only he can make. The situation is probably commonest when dealing with

6 Letter from architect to client if asked to tender on fees

Dear Sir

[*insert appropriate heading*]

Thank you for your letter of [*insert date*].

I am pleased to hear that you are considering appointing me as architect for the above project. The RIBA Code of Professional Conduct lays down criteria which I must satisfy before quoting a fee. In particular, the precise nature and scope of the work must be known together with the services required. Presumably these will pose no problems in this instance.

Naturally, you are most welcome to visit me to discuss the work or, alternatively, you might find it more convenient to meet me at the proposed site. I can supply you with details of some of the jobs undertaken by this office so that you can visit and see the kind of work done. May I suggest that you telephone me to arrange a meeting.

A copy of *Standard Form of Agreement for the Appointment of an Architect* is enclosed so that you can form an idea of the services you require.

Yours faithfully

7 Letter from architect to client if decisions late

Dear Sir

[*insert appropriate heading*]

I refer to my letter/telephone call [*omit as appropriate*] of [*insert date*] requesting [*briefly indicate the decision required*].

It would be appreciated if you would review your arrangements for providing urgent decisions in the interests of avoiding delays and extra costs.

I am sure you will appreciate that, although I am always ready to give you the benefit of my professional advice, there are certain points which must be referred to you.

Yours faithfully

8 Letter from architect to client if he is reluctant to make a decision

Dear Sir

[*insert appropriate heading*]

Thank you for your letter of [*insert date*].

Naturally, I will give you every professional assistance I can, but there are certain decisions which are, effectively, your instructions to me. Obviously I cannot instruct myself, and, without instructions, I am unable to carry out my professional duty.

In previous letters I have set out the considerations which you should take into account, and there may be others of which you alone are aware. If it will be of assistance, the instruction required can be put simply as follows:

[*Put the decision required as briefly and succinctly as possible in the form of a clear question which can be answered by a straightforward 'yes' or 'no'.*]

I look forward to hearing from you as soon as possible. A delay is now occurring which it could be difficult to make up and will increase the ultimate cost of the project.

Yours faithfully

a client who is actually a board of directors, even though they may have agreed that one of their number is to liaise with you.

This situation can arise at any time during the work, but you should identify the signs at the earliest possible moment – i.e. as soon as a decision is late – and take immediate action.

There are a number of important points you have noted in the letter:

- ❏ The date you requested instructions
- ❏ The fact that you are still waiting
- ❏ Possible delays and additional costs
- ❏ Your willingness to give professional advice
- ❏ The fact that there are certain decisions you cannot make

If your client is one person, a businessman for example, he will almost certainly grasp the points immediately and send you his decision by return. Difficulties sometimes continue if your client is a body of people – a large company, local authority, government department, etc. Much depends upon the calibre of your liaison.

If in spite of your letter, the client replies in some such manner as: 'I leave it to you to use your professional judgment in the matter', beware; what he is really saying is: 'I cannot make up my mind and I would like you to do it for me and take the blame if the decision is wrong'.

He is inviting you to make the decision yourself. It is very tempting to do just that if the matter is urgent and money is being lost. You must resist the temptation because he is giving you no indemnity if the decision is wrong – quite the reverse. He is telling you that he expects you to take responsibility for a decision (which should be his) as part of your normal professional duties. The precise terms of your reply will vary depending upon the nature of the decision and your knowledge of the client. Letter 8 is intended as an example.

If your client continues to evade the question, you must visit him and discuss the matter thoroughly. Persist in requiring his immediate decision and, on your return to the office, confirm his instructions back to him in polite but clear terms.

A5 Consultants: client requiring them to be appointed through the architect (9), (10), (11)

Where the work is such that consultants are required, you will advise your client accordingly. From a contractual point of view, the client should appoint consultants directly. However, your client may understandably feel that he wishes to deal with only one professional

9 Letter from architect to client regarding direct appointment of consultants

Dear Sir

[*insert appropriate heading*]

I refer to our recent conversation regarding the necessity to appoint consultants for [*list services*]. I understand that you wish me to appoint consultants for this project through my office.

It is of course, perfectly possible to do as you suggest, but it would be against my advice. I will, in any case, co-ordinate all consultancy services. Clauses 4.1.1 to 4.1.8 inclusive of the conditions of the *Standard Form of Agreement for the Appointment of an Architect* set out the relevant points. Consultancy fees are the same whether appointed directly or through my office.

I strongly advise you to consider appointing the consultants directly yourself. It is usual practice in construction projects and enables you to have direct access to the other professionals as the work proceeds. I would carry out preliminary negotiations with each consultant and advise you regarding appointment.

However, the normal practice in construction projects is that the client appoints his own consultants. By so doing, you have direct access to the other professionals should you so wish and, of course, direct recourse to them for any problems which may arise.

Please give this matter further thought and I look forward to hearing from you within the next few days.

Yours faithfully

10 Letter from architect to client if architect is to appoint consultants

Dear Sir

[*insert appropriate heading*]

Thank you for your letter of [*insert date*] in which you instruct me to engage the services of consultants on your behalf. I shall be happy to act as agent for you in this matter. The appointments are now in hand.

May I take this opportunity of drawing your attention to clause 4.1.7 of the conditions of the RIBA *Standard Form of Agreement for the Appointment of an Architect*, a copy of which is in your possession, which provides that you will hold each consultant responsible for the competence, general inspection and performance of the work entrusted to him.

Yours faithfully

11 Letter from architect to consultant seeking indemnity

Dear Sir

[*insert appropriate heading*]

I refer to recent discussions regarding your employment as consultant for [*name services*] on the above project.

Before a formal contract of engagement can be drawn up, I require you to provide me with proof that you carry and will continue to carry suitable and adequate professional indemnity insurance. Please signify your willingness to indemnify me against any claims which may be made in respect of the competence, general inspection and performance of work entrusted to you.

Yours faithfully

to avoid confusion. He may ask you to deal with every aspect of the project yourself, including the appointment of consultants. You must try to persuade him to appoint directly and set the matter on record **(9)**.

If the client is adamant that you should provide consultant's services through your office and you agree, you must make sure that:

❏ You appoint consultants as your client's agent with his agreement **(10)**
❏ The consultants' contract with you reflects the terms of your contract with your client
❏ You have your client's agreement to pay the appropriate additional fees to cover consultant's services
❏ You obtain an indemnity from the consultant and check that he has proper insurance cover to back up any claims made against him **(11)**
❏ Your own professional indemnity insurers are aware of the arrangements

Do not place unlimited faith in clause 4.1.7 of the conditions in the *Standard Form of Agreement for the Appointment of an Architect* and expect that the client will always seek redress from the consultant direct. You are always the most likely first candidate for your client's displeasure in whatever form it may come. The problem is, of course, that if for some reason your client cannot recover damages from the consultant, you may be faced with the liability yourself.

Other than the first, the above criteria apply with even more force if you offer your client an 'all in' service by engaging consultants as and when you require them. You must always ensure that your client is aware if you intend to delegate work in this way.

A6 Other architects, if previously commissioned (12), (13)

When asked to take a commission, there is always the possibility that another architect may have been engaged by the client upon the same work. Principle 3, rule 3.5 of the RIBA Code of Professional Conduct requires you to notify such an architect if you know of his engagement or if you can so discover by reasonable enquiry.

There are two stages:

❏ Discover if another architect has been engaged
❏ Write to the other architect

Your letter to the client can be part of another letter or can stand on

12 Letter from architect to client regarding other architects

Dear Sir

[*insert appropriate heading*]

The code of professional conduct requires me to make reasonable enquiries to discover if you have previously engaged any other architect upon the above work. If so, perhaps you will let me have his name and address so that I may inform him of my involvement.

Yours faithfully

13   Letter from architect to other architects regarding former engagement

Dear Sir

[*insert appropriate heading*]

I have been approached/instructed [*omit as appropriate*] by [*insert name of client*] to undertake the above work.

I understand that you were engaged upon this project at one time.

Please take this as notice in accordance with principle 3, rule 3.5 of the RIBA Code of Professional Conduct.

Yours faithfully

its own. Being able to show that you have made reasonable inquiry will often avoid future unpleasantness.

The other architect may simply acknowledge, ignore or state formally that he has no objections. In any case, you have complied with your obligations in regard to him.

The position is complicated if he makes particular comments. He may say, for example, that he was never paid. Besides being a useful indication of your own chances of obtaining fees, it is good practice to request your client to discharge previous fees before you take his instructions. You have no duty to do this and, if previous fees are the subject of court proceedings or simply in dispute, you would be advised to stand back and make no comments of any kind.

In such a case, however, you would be wise to consider whether you wish to proceed until the previous case is settled. It is not your place, indeed it would be inappropriate for you, to pass moral judgments on disputes with which you are not involved, but it may not auger well for your own relations with the client. If you do proceed, a payment on account (as in A1) would appear to be advisable.

A7 Site boundaries: unclear (14), (15)

It is not at all unusual to find that one or more of your client's site boundaries is not clearly defined either on site or on the deeds. It is not part of your normal duty to settle such matters.

If full information is not provided, you may be tempted to carry out your survey anyway using your common sense to fix the boundaries. Resist the temptation. The client must provide you with all necessary information. If it becomes necessary to negotiate with adjoining owners to fix the boundaries, this is best done by the client's solicitor. If you are asked to take part in the negotiations, you are entitled to request an additional fee for your services and you should make the position clear to your client.

14 Letter from architect to client if site boundary not clear

Dear Sir

[*insert appropriate heading*]

I have inspected the above site in a general manner today. Parts of the boundary are not clear. I have looked at the deeds and they shed no light on the matter.

Before I carry out a detailed survey, it is essential that the limits of your ownership are properly defined.

A rough sketch plan of the area is enclosed, noting the principal features – walls, roads, adjacent buildings etc. Perhaps you would be good enough to ask your solicitor to indicate the precise extent of your ownership by drawing a red line around the site and returning the sketch to me as soon as possible. Please show dimensions if available.

Yours faithfully

15 Letter from architect to client if requested to help in boundary negotiations

Dear Sir

[*insert appropriate heading*]

Thank you for your letter of [*insert date*].

I will be happy to assist in the negotiations with adjoining owners in order to fix the site boundaries. Your own solicitor should take charge of the negotiations and I will be present to advise at any meetings between all parties.

An additional fee at the rate of [*insert amount*] per hour is chargeable for such additional services, and I should be pleased to have your agreement. Clause 1.5.7 of the conditions of the RIBA *Standard Form of Agreement for the Appointment of an Architect* refers.

Perhaps you will ask your solicitor to telephone me directly to arrange a meeting.

Yours faithfully

B Feasibility

B1 Brief: unacceptable requirements (16)

A considerable degree of tact is required to obtain a proper brief from your client. At this stage it must be neither too detailed nor too general.

It is not unusual for a client involved in building for the first time to attempt to impose requirements which are basically whims. The ideas may be so fixed in his mind, however, that he refuses to consider a design unless they are incorporated. A parish priest may have a longing for Gothic arches in his new church, a managing director may require a symmetrical elevation to his office block, the private housebuilder dormers on his roof. Such requirements are usually completely irrelevant and show a lack of understanding of the architect's true function. You can, of course, resign your commission but that is a drastic step, hardly justified. If you produce a good design, the client will usually realise his initial mistake himself and be happy to forget his particular obsession as he becomes involved with the excellent way in which you have interpreted his requirements. In the meantime, send him a tactful letter.

B2 Existing property, if urgent repair work required (17)

During your survey of existing property, it may become clear that certain works must be carried out urgently if the integrity of the fabric is to be preserved. As soon as this becomes apparent, you should waste no time in informing your client and obtaining his instructions. Telephone him first and follow up with a letter.

Your client will be unhappy about the prospect of signing a blank cheque, and it may well be possible for you to obtain some indication, with the assistance of the quantity surveyor and the firm in question, of the likely cost. Much depends upon the urgency of the situation, and your letter should be amended accordingly.

16   Letter from architect to client who has unacceptable requirements

Dear Sir

[*insert appropriate heading*]

I refer to our discussion of [*insert date*] during which your general requirements were noted.

I am proceeding with the feasibility study. If it proves acceptable to you, I will prepare outline proposals for your consideration.

I realise that you are anxious to include [*insert the disputed feature*] and I suggest that, while bearing that in mind, we allow the design to take shape in a purely logical way at first and review the situation at outline proposal stage, when we will have a better understanding of the way the building is developing.

Yours faithfully

17 Letter from architect to client if urgent repairs required

Dear Sir

[*insert appropriate heading*]

I refer to our telephone conversation of [*insert date*].

During our survey of the above property, it was discovered that [*insert description of the problem as clearly as possible*].

In order to avoid the possibility of collapse [*or insert the appropriate danger*] I strongly advise that immediate work is necessary.

In view of the nature and urgency of the work, it is impossible to obtain competitive quotations. I request your agreement to the employment of [*insert name of a suitable contractor or specialist firm*] to carry out the necessary work on site.

If you give me authority to employ on your behalf the above firm, or some other firm which you may care to nominate, I will instruct them to carry out the necessary work and request them to submit accounts directly to you for payment.

Yours faithfully

C Outline Proposals

C1 Objections: by client (18)

Undoubtedly, the best way to submit outline proposals is to take them personally to your client and explain them thoroughly. Unless he is an unusually decisive person, he will normally wish to study the proposals and possibly discuss them with his colleagues. In due course you can expect to receive his comments and sometimes objections to some aspects of your scheme.

If you have done your job properly, the comments should be constructive and the objections minor. If the points are all reasonable, you should have little difficulty in revising your proposals to satisfy them.

A problem arises if you consider any objection on the part of the client to be unreasonable. You should revise your scheme as required except for the unreasonable objection and marshall your arguments in the most convincing way.

When faced with your proposals, revised to suit his comments except in one particular, you should have little difficulty in persuading your client of the soundness of your own thinking – provided you have done your homework. Resist any attempt to discuss the problem on the telephone. A face-to-face discussion over the drawings is much more likely to yield fruitful results.

C2 Objections: by planning authority, civic society etc. (19), (20), (21)

At this stage in the project a number of bodies may register objections. The local planning authority is the most obvious, and, in order to achieve the scheme you want, you may be engaged in a considerable amount of discussion. They have their own criteria when confronted with proposals, and some of their concerns may not be yours. Generally, however, they are very helpful in trying to reach a solution.

Avoid a head-on confrontation: it only leads to entrenched positions and eventual refusal. See what can be agreed so as gradually to isolate

18 Letter from architect to client if objection unreasonable

Dear Sir

[*insert appropriate heading*]

Thank you for your useful comments on the outline proposals for the above project.

Most of your suggestions have posed no problems and they have been incorporated in revised proposals.

Only one point has proved difficult to reconcile with the brief as a whole: [*outline the point in question*].

I suggest that the best way to solve the problem is for me to visit you for a thorough discussion. I will telephone you within the next day or so to arrange a suitable time and date.

Yours faithfully

19 Letter from architect to planning authority after objections

Dear Sir

[*insert appropriate heading*]

I refer to discussions in your department held with [*insert names of the appropriate planning officers*] on [*insert date/s*].

In accordance with the agreement reached at the above meeting(s), I have revised the proposals and enclose [*insert number of drawings they require*] sets of drawings numbers [*insert numbers*]. I understand that you will insert them in place of the original drawings numbers [*insert numbers*] for the consideration of your committee.

Thank you for your co-operation in this matter and I look forward to your approval on [*insert date on which they have agreed to confirm their decision*].

If there are any further last-minute points arising, I should appreciate a telephone call to resolve them as speedily as possible.

Yours faithfully

20 Letter from architect to client regarding amenity society objections

Dear Sir

[*insert appropriate heading*]

I refer to our telephone conversation of [*insert date*] and confirm that you are in agreement with my suggestion that I should address the [*insert name of society*] members on the subject of the above proposals. The meeting will take place on [*insert date*] at [*insert time*] and I will report the result to you as soon as possible.

[*If your client has commodious premises and he has agreed that the meeting should be held there, write the following instead:*]

I refer to our telephone conversation of [*insert date*] and confirm that you are in agreement with my suggestion that I should address [*insert name of society*] members at your premises on [*insert date*] at [*insert time*], the subject being the above project.

If you can arrange some light refreshments, a pleasant relaxed atmosphere should be possible in which we ought to be able to convince them that we share their concern for environmental issues.

Yours faithfully

21 Letter from architect to amenity society if they have objections

Dear Sir

[*insert appropriate heading*]

I refer to your letter of [*insert date*] and our telephone conversation of [*insert date*].

[*Add <u>one</u> of the following paragraphs:*]

I confirm that I will be delighted to attend a meeting of your members on [*insert date*] at [*insert time*] in the [*insert venue*] to speak and answer questions about the above project. I will bring illustrative material with me.

I confirm that my client has extended a warm invitation to your members, which I understand you accept, to visit his premises on [*insert date*] at [*insert time*] when I will speak and answer questions on the above project. Illustrative material will be on display. The address of my client's premises is [*insert address*]. Please let me know the approximate number you expect to attend.

Yours faithfully

the main problems. A little patience and diplomacy coupled with a professed understanding of the authority's problems will often succeed in reducing the objection itself to a mere detail. The objections of the planning authority can sometimes be used, if all else fails, to convince the client to see the solution your way. After agreement, always send a revised set of drawings (as many copies as individual authorities require) in confirmation.

Civic societies, amenity groups and the like are a much more subtle problem. Some architects believe that the best policy is to ignore them, but that can be a grave error. They wield great influence, and if you receive an objection from them, the best policy is often to offer to visit the group with plans and models (if possible) and explain the project. It is really a public relations exercise which should not be missed. Once you have shown your interest in their particular concerns, their objections often melt away. Get your client's approval first.

It is easiest to discuss the arrangements with your client and the amenity group by telephone and then confirm by letter. The letters will obviously vary slightly but **20** and **21** can be considered guides.

After the meeting, confirm the results to your client and, if the objections have been withdrawn, to the society to avoid future dispute.

D Scheme Design

D1 Client, if no reply (22)

It may happen that, after you have produced your scheme design and presented it to your client for consideration and approval, you hear nothing from him for some time. Exactly how long you should wait before taking some action depends on circumstances. When you left your scheme with him, you should have obtained some idea of the time he would need for consideration. He may, for example, wish to discuss it with someone who is on holiday or he may wish to present it to a meeting of the Board of Directors – although you should ask to present it yourself at any such meeting.

After taking everything into consideration, you may feel that your client should have written or telephoned his approval or comments. It is best not to telephone him without warning. An unexpected telephone call can be unwelcome and provoke a hurried response. A letter is more likely to produce a better reply particularly if you make it clear that you intend to telephone later.

D2 Client, if another architect appointed to continue work (23), (24), (25)

The client is entitled to terminate your appointment at any time if he gives you reasonable notice and pays any fees due. There are two important factors to consider:

❑ Your copyright on the designs
❑ The appointment of another architect

Assuming that the RIBA *Standard Form of Agreement for the Appointment of an Architect* (SFA 92) is part of your agreement, the client will be entitled to use your designs provided you have completed stage D and he has paid all outstanding fees. If stage D has not been completed, you are entitled to negotiate with your former client for the use of your designs. This might involve the payment of some appro-

22 Letter from architect to client if no reply

Dear Sir

[*insert appropriate heading*]

We have reached an important stage in this project and I understand your wish to be certain that the scheme satisfies your requirements as fully as possible.

Much more preparatory work has to be done before operations can commence on site. If we can expedite this work, it should result, ultimately, in a lower contract price. At the moment, I am awaiting your comments on the scheme design which was left with you on [*insert date*]. May I ask you to let me have your approval or comments as soon as possible?

I will telephone in a day or so to discuss the current position.

Yours faithfully

23 Letter from architect to client if services terminated

Dear Sir

[*insert appropriate heading*]

Thank you for your letter of [*insert date*].

I note that you wish to terminate my services on the above project. It is normal practice, in these circumstances, to give reasonable notice because it is difficult to bring work to an abrupt halt and relocate staff. I am, however, arranging to stop all further work on your project as soon as possible. An account to cover all outstanding fees is enclosed for your attention. When I receive payment, you will be entitled to all the drawings and documents prepared for the work although, due to the abruptness of the termination, the information will be incomplete and I cannot accept any responsibility for errors or omissions. It will be your responsibility to appoint another architect to thoroughly check through and complete the production information.

[*Add one of the following paragraphs: (A) if Stage D has been completed or you are charging full recommended fees, (B) if Stage D has not been completed or you are charging a nominal fee:*]

(A) On payment of my fees, you are entitled to make use of the design, once only, on the site to which it relates. The copyright in all the documents remains my property.

(B) You are not entitled to reproduce my designs by executing the project without my permission. I am prepared to grant you permission to reproduce my design, once only, on the site to which it relates on payment of an additional fee of [*insert amount*]. The copyright in all the documents remains my property.

Yours faithfully

24   Letter from architect to client if another architect appointed

Dear Sir

[*insert appropriate heading*]

I have been informed that you have appointed another architect to carry out the above project. Perhaps you would be good enough to confirm whether my information is correct?

My own appointment continues until you formally give me reasonable notice of termination. At that point I would prepare my fee account.

I look forward to hearing from you as soon as possible so that I can make the necessary preparations to stop work.

Yours faithfully

25 Letter from architect to another architect appointed by client

Dear Sir

[*insert appropriate heading*]

I have been informed that my client [*insert name*] has instructed you to carry out work on the above project. Since I have not had any communication from you in accordance with principle 3, rule 3.5 of the RIBA Code of Professional Conduct, I should be pleased if you would let me know whether my information is correct.

I have also written to my client, informing him that my appointment is not terminated until I receive reasonable notice of termination, at which point I will submit my fee account.

Obviously, I accept that you were not aware of my prior involvement but, if you have accepted my client's instructions, I should be grateful if you would inform him that it would not be proper for you to proceed until the appropriate termination formalities have been completed.

Yours faithfully

priate additional fee. You should not withhold your consent unreasonably; for example, simply because you feel annoyed at the termination of your appointment. (If the SFA 92 has not been used, the general rule appears to be that, if you have charged the full recommended fee for the work you have done at the time of termination, your client has paid for a licence to use your designs.)

If the client appoints a new architect, he should inform you of the fact. Most of the problems which arise from this situation can be traced to vagueness in the original appointment and failure to sign a proper agreement incorporating the terms of the SFA 92. If this is the case, you should write to your client as soon as he informs you that your services are no longer required **(23)**.

If you simply hear that another architect has been appointed and you receive no communication from either client or architect (it does happen), you should write to both parties **(24)**, **(25)**.

D3 Client, if preference expressed for a particular sub-contractor (26)

If your client wishes to use a particular sub-contractor on a contract it usually implies nomination. If the sub-contractor is suitable, there is no particular problem except that you might advise your client that it would be advisable to obtain competitive tenders. A problem arises if the sub-contractor is, in your opinion, unsuitable. There could be a number of reasons, among them:

❏ Too large or small to do the work
❏ Too inexperienced
❏ Your past experience has shown him to be unreliable or a poor workman

Your client should accept your advice, but he may not (the sub-contractor may be a friend or relative). After using your powers of persuasion to no avail and warning him of the possible consequences, confirm your views in writing to protect yourself in the future.

D4 Client: objection to the use of sub-contractor or supplier in a design capacity (27)

A sub-contractor or supplier is often used in a design capacity, for example, to design a lift installation. It is usual, in such cases, to arrange for a form of warranty or for an employer/nominated sub-

26 Letter from architect to client regarding unsuitable sub-contractor

Dear Sir

[*insert appropriate heading*]

I refer to our discussion of [*insert date*] regarding the employment of [*insert name*] for sub-contract [*insert type of work*] works on the above contract and I confirm the following:

[*select appropriate points*]

1   You instructed me to obtain competitive tenders from three firms including [*insert name*] for the above sub-contract works.

[or]

1   You instructed me to obtain a tender from only one firm, [*insert name*], for the above sub-contract works.

2   I have advised you that, in my opinion, this firm is not suitable for the work.

3   I have further advised you that, if the firm is nominated to do the work, the consequences to the contract could be far-reaching in terms of additional expense, delays in progress and completion and the quality of workmanship and materials.

4   If you insist, I will carry out your instructions but I can take no responsibility for the outcome because it is against my direct advice. As soon as the contract is signed, I must carry out my duty to administer the contract provisions fairly between the parties.

Please consider the matter once again and let me have your final instructions as soon as possible.

Yours faithfully

27   Letter from architect to client if he objects to supplier or sub-contractor used in a design capacity

Dear Sir

[*insert appropriate heading*]

Thank you for your letter of [*insert date*]. I can understand your concern and hasten to reassure you.

The various consultants' fees are based only on the work they do. Therefore, any design work attributable to suppliers or to sub-contractors is excluded. I have proposed the present method of proceeding because the particular services offered by the supplier/sub-contractor [*omit as appropriate*] will be much cheaper than to commission a design by consultants and then have it carried out by the main contractor. This is because a number of suppliers/sub-contractors [*omit as appropriate*] have their own patented systems which they have refined over a number of years. There is a system of warranties and agreements to protect your interest in the event of a design failure.

I trust that I have allayed your fears and that you will signify your agreement to the employment of suppliers and sub-contractors [*use only one term if appropriate*] in a design capacity on this project.

Yours faithfully

contractor form of agreement to be completed in the case of a nominated sub-contractor. Naturally, the client must be informed of your intentions. He may object on the grounds that you are supposed to be responsible for the design and he is already paying additional fees to consultants; therefore, surely all the design should be carried out by his professional advisors. You will have to write and explain.

E Detail Design

E1 Client: wishing to modify brief (28), (29)

Although you will have impressed upon your client the need for *final* briefing decisions at stage D, it is likely that he will ask for some alterations at a later stage. 'Will you increase the car parking provisions from twenty to twenty-five cars?' is the sort of request which may be irritating but not catastrophic to the scheme as a whole. Late requests to alter the brief in a minor way are probably best acknowledged with a gentle reminder of timing. Alterations having a major effect require you to inform your client of the serious consequences. You must, as always, adjust the precise wording to suit the type of client.

28 Letter from architect to client if he wishes to make minor modifications to the brief

Dear Sir

[*insert appropriate heading*]

Thank you for your letter of [*insert date*] requesting me to [*insert a note of the alterations required*]. The work has been put in hand.

Although the alterations are minor, they will require a certain amount of re-drawing, re-scheduling and liaison with consultants.

I know, from our previous conversations, that you appreciate the problems caused by quite small changes of mind and the possible repercussions in terms of cost and programme time. Obviously, the problems become more serious as the work of the design team progresses further.

Yours faithfully

Copy: Quantity surveyor

29 Letter from architect to client if he wishes to make major modifications to the brief

Dear Sir

[*insert appropriate heading*]

Thank you for your letter of [*insert date*] requesting me to [*insert a note of the alterations required*]. The work has been put in hand but your decision to change the brief at this late stage causes me concern on your behalf.

A considerable amount of work already completed must be amended, including liaison with consultants. It is now very unlikely that the date originally envisaged for commencement on site can be achieved.

I have asked the quantity surveyor to revise the cost estimates for you in the light of your latest requirements. Additional fees will be due to cover the extra work, and the consultants may also request additional fees.

May I very strongly reinforce what I have said in our previous conversations, that alterations in the brief at this stage can be very expensive in time and money? Obviously, as work progresses, alterations becoming increasingly time-consuming and costly.

Yours faithfully

Copy: Quantity surveyor

F Production Information

F1 Client: declines to use a standard contract (30)

Your client may consider the JCT Standard Form of Contract excessively complicated. He may require you to use a simpler form of contract; possibly he wishes his own solicitor to draft an agreement. It may be that some variations of the Standard Form, such as the Intermediate Form or the Minor Works Form, would be appropriate, or it may be that a different procurement system is indicated, such as management contracting, construction management or design and build. If so, try to persuade him to use it. If not or if he refuses to use it, put the facts down in writing.

F2 Client: wishes to include unsuitable contractor on tender list (31)

If your client asks you to include on the list of tenderers, a contractor whom you know to be unsuitable, make the point to him very strongly. It is probably best to reserve your precise comments for oral communication. If your client insists, it might even be worthwhile relinquishing your commission rather than face the certainty of continuous dispute. It is too much to expect your client to thank you if you make a stand; but he will certainly blame you later if you do not. Your letter is, to some extent, a variation of the letter in D3.

F3 Client: asks you to recommend a contractor (32)

Your client may say that he understands nothing about building and that he would like you to recommend suitable contractors for inclusion on the tender list. Presumably you have carried out the checks

30 Letter from architect to client if he declines to use a standard contract

Dear Sir

[*insert appropriate heading*]

I refer to our recent conversations regarding the use of the JCT Standard Form of Building Contract. I appreciate that you find it long and complex and I understand why you think that a form of contract, drafted by your own solicitor, would be preferable. Before you come to a firm decision, however, I would ask you to consider the following:

1 The Standard Form of Building Contract 1980 was produced by the joint contracts tribunal after many years of experiencing the operation of the Contract in practice. It is designed to cater for virtually every eventuality which might arise during the course of building works of the kind you envisage.

2 The joint contracts tribunal is composed of representatives of all sections of the building industry, including architects and lawyers. As a result, the standard form is widely recognised throughout the industry and its implications clearly understood by architect and contractor alike.

3 Contractors have a marked reluctance to tender other than on a standard form and, therefore, the use of a completely new form would result in increased tender prices as contractors attempt to allow for the unknown. It is possible that contractors will refuse to tender.

4 It is part of my duty to understand the contract and interpret it fairly between the parties.

I have to advise you about the most suitable form of contract for your purpose and to assist you in completion. If you have objections to specific parts, I will explain the implications to you. If you wish, I can obtain expert advice. This would be done best at a meeting and I will telephone you in a few days when you have had the opportunity to consider this letter.

Yours faithfully

31 Letter from architect to client if he wishes to include unsuitable contractor on tender list

Dear Sir

[*insert appropriate heading*]

Thank you for your letter of [*insert date*]. I note that you wish me to include [*insert name*] on the tender list.

This contractor is well known to me and I do not consider him suitable to carry out the above work.

I am, of course, prepared to explain my reasons more fully on the telephone or at a meeting. I trust, however, that it will not be necessary and you will confirm your agreement to exclude this particular contractor on this occasion.

Yours faithfully

32 Letter from architect to client if asked to recommend a contractor

Dear Sir

[*insert appropriate heading*]

I refer to our recent telephone conversation when you asked me to recommend some contractors for inclusion on the tender list for this project.

Naturally, I will do everything I can to assist. Recommendation of contractors is not something which falls within the scope of my professional duties. What I can do is to carry out the checks suggested in the *Code of Procedure for Single Stage Selective Tendering 1994*. I have carried out those checks in respect of the contractors listed on the attached sheet and the results are also enclosed. They indicate that each of the contractors appears capable of executing the works to the required standard and you will note the remarks in the references I have obtained. Although you have the final decision, I shall be happy to discuss your choices in the light of these results. Perhaps you will telephone me when you have had the opportunity to consider the matter.

Yours faithfully

suggested in the *Code of Procedure for Single Stage Selective Tendering 1994* and asked for references from other architects. Even though these checks may indicate that each of your proposed tenderers are firms of the highest calibre with impeccable financial pedigrees, you should on no account recommend any of them. Architects have been successfully sued for doing so if the contractor subsequently renders poor service. You cannot guarantee the contractor and you are not called upon to do so by your conditions of engagement.

F4 Client: reluctance to appoint a full-time clerk of works (33)

Your client may sometimes resist the appointment of a full-time clerk of works. It may be because he does not realise the significance of having constant inspection of certain jobs. Some large organisations have their own clerks of works permanently employed. In those cases, the organisation may not wish to commit a clerk of works full-time upon the site.

The employment of a full-time clerk of works will not relieve you of your obligations to your client. Indeed, an inefficient clerk of works could add to your difficulties. It is very much in your interests that your client does appoint a clerk of works because it may reduce your liability for damages if the worst happens. However, if you recommend the appointment of a full-time clerk of works and your client is unwilling to agree, you should do what you can to safeguard your position.

MW 80

It is unusual for a clerk of works to be appointed, and there is no provision in the conditions. Provisions can be made for a clerk of works in the specification, however, if the size or complexity of the works warrant it.

F5 Consultants, if late in supplying drawings and specification (34)

You will have prepared a programme at a meeting of the design team to ensure that all production information is ready on time. If some information from consultants is not available at the right time, you should lose no time in telephoning to hurry things along. Obtain a

33 Letter from architect to client if reluctant to appoint full-time clerk of works

Dear Sir

[*insert appropriate heading*]

Thank you for your letter of [*insert date*] and I note that you think it unnecessary to appoint a full-time clerk of works upon the above contract.

In some contracts of limited value a clerk of works is clearly unnecessary. However, this contract does not fall into that category.[1] The conditions under which I am engaged to carry out this work are the RIBA *Standard Form of Agreement for the Appointment of an Architect* and, in accordance with clause 3.1.1, I notified you in writing of the visits I expected to make. This was on the basis that a clerk of works would be employed on site and I have so advised in accordance with clause 3.3.1. I strongly advise you to reconsider your decision. The employment of a clerk of works is likely to repay his cost several times over in savings on lost time and money as the contract progresses.

Although, naturally, I will carry out my own duties punctiliously, on a contract of this size[2] I cannot accept responsibility for failure to notice such defects as would be discovered by a full-time clerk of works.

Yours faithfully

---

[1] *Omit the first two sentences when using MW 80*
[2] *Substitute 'this type' on MW 80*

34 Letter from architect to consultant if information late

Dear Sir

[*insert appropriate heading*]

According to the programme of work agreed by all members of the design team, you should have delivered [*indicate nature of information*] to this office on [*insert date*] at latest.

I telephoned your Mr [*insert name*] on [*insert date*] and he promised to get the information to me by [*insert date*]. I have received nothing by this morning's post.

The position now is that a substantial portion of my own work has been delayed by [*insert number of days or weeks*]. The consequences in cost and delay are unacceptable to our mutual client and he is unwilling to absorb my additional fees. I should be pleased to receive, by return, all programmed information and your assurance that no further delays will occur.

Yours faithfully

definite delivery promise. If the information is still delayed, confirm the situation in writing.

F6 Sub-contractor or supplier, if tender not on standard form or conditions attached (35), (36)

You will have required tenders on the appropriate standard forms from all proposed nominated sub-contractors or suppliers. It is not unusual for either the standard form to be ignored and tenders submitted on the firm's own form, or the standard form to be submitted with the firm's special conditions attached.

You cannot consider either tender. Basically, three courses of action are open to you:

- ❏ Exclude the tender from consideration
- ❏ Request the firm to resubmit on the proper form **(35)**
- ❏ Request the firm to withdraw their special condition **(36)**

F7 Sub-contractor or supplier, if price too high (37)

You may find that the lowest acceptable tender for a particular item of sub-contract works or supply is higher than your estimate in the overall cost plan prepared for the project. There can be many reasons for this, only one of which is an error in the initial estimate. If sufficient money can be found in other parts of the cost plan to make up the difference without the danger of lowering standards, there should be no problem, although it is always wise to inform your client that the tender exceeded the allowance.

Difficulties arise if the difference is too great and the total cost is likely to be increased. Do not attempt to cover up the problem. Your client will be disappointed but, most of all, he will want advice. Give it to him; he may think the fault is yours. Be defensive and he will be sure the fault is yours.

In the letter you have carried out your duty exactly by informing your client, at the earliest possible moment, of the possibility of overspending. It gives him the opportunity of giving you any fresh instructions he may think appropriate. You have also confirmed that you are proceeding and, in effect, you are advising him to stay calm until he sees the total main tender figure.

35 Letter from architect to sub-contractor or supplier if tender improperly submitted 1

Dear Sir

[*insert appropriate heading*]

I have received your tender for [*insert type of work or materials*] in connection with the above contract.

The tender cannot be considered in its present form. If you wish to be considered, please complete the standard form of tender, a further two copies of which are enclosed, and return it to me not later than [*insert date and time*].

Please note that the submission of the tender on your own form or the inclusion of your own special conditions, other than in the appropriate place on the standard form, will result in disqualification.

Yours faithfully

36 Letter from architect to sub-contractor or supplier if tender improperly submitted 2

Dear Sir

[*insert appropriate heading*]

I have received your tender for [*insert type of work or materials*] in connection with the above contract.

If you wish your tender to be considered, you must inform me in writing by [*insert date*] that you withdraw the conditions [*specify conditions*] while maintaining your offer price of £ [*insert price in tender*] unchanged. If you do not feel able to agree to this course of action, your tender will not be considered.

Yours faithfully

37 Letter from architect to client if sub-contractor's or supplier's price is too high

Dear Sir

[*insert appropriate heading*]

We have received tenders for [*indicate the item of work*]. The lowest acceptable tender amounted to [*state the sum*]. The sum allowed in the cost plan was [*state the sum*]. The difference is greater than the total savings on the rest of the prime cost sums by a margin of [*state the sum*]. In my opinion we are unlikely to achieve a lower price by inviting new tenders. At this stage the indication is that the total estimate for the works will be exceeded by [*state the sum*]. Obviously, it is not possible to say what the lowest tender figure for the main contract will be.

To attempt to achieve savings at this stage may be misguided because some lowering of standards would be involved which could prove to be unnecessary. Unless you instruct me to the contrary, therefore, I will proceed with my work, and, when the main contract tenders are received, we can review the situation together if the estimated total cost is exceeded.

Yours faithfully

Copy: Quantity surveyor

F8 Letters of intent to sub-contractors or suppliers (38)

You may feel that it is desirable to have sub-contract design carried out, to have shop drawings produced or even to put certain work in hand before the main contract is let. The procedure is usually carried out by means of a letter of intent. The process is fraught with difficulties:

- ❏ The main contractor, when appointed, may object to the nominated sub-contractor unless you have named him in the main contract tender documents
- ❏ The client will be faced with certain costs even if the project does not proceed
- ❏ The courts sometimes consider that letters of intent create a full binding contract
- ❏ If the whole, or substantially the whole of the sub-contract work is carried out on the basis of a letter of intent, the sub-contractor would be entitled to payment on the basis of *quantum meruit* (a reasonable sum – defined as a 'fair commercial rate'). It could amount to considerably more than the sub-contract tender figure, particularly in times of keen tendering.

The inescapable conclusion is that letters of intent should be avoided. If you must send one, make sure that you get your client's written approval and that he is fully aware of the implications. He must see your letter and agree its terms before you send it. It is probably not going too far to suggest that every letter of intent should be scrutinised by an expert contract consultant before being despatched.

38 Letter from architect to sub-contractor or supplier: letter of intent

Dear Sir

[*insert appropriate heading*]

My client, [*insert name*], has instructed me to inform you that your tender of the [*insert date*] in the sum of [*insert amount in figures and words*] for [*insert the nature of the works*] is acceptable and that I intend to instruct the main contractor to tender into a sub-contract[1] with you after the main contract has been signed.

It is not my client's intention that this letter, taken alone or in conjunction with your tender, should form a binding contract. However, my client is prepared to instruct you to [*insert the limited nature of the work required*]. If, for any reason whatsoever, the project does not proceed, my client's commitment will be strictly limited to payment for [*insert the limited nature of the work required*].

No other work[2] included in your tender must be carried out without further written order. No further obligation is placed upon my client and no obligation whatever, under any circumstances, is placed upon me.

Yours faithfully

---

[1] *Substitute 'place an order' in the case of a supplier*
[2] *Substitute 'work or materials' in the case of a supplier*

G Bills of Quantities

Note: This section will not be required if it is proposed to use JCT 80 or IFC 84 Without Quantities or MW 80.

G1 Drawings, if not ready

The quantity surveyor requires all drawings and other production information to be complete before he begins to take off quantities. In practice, it very rarely works out so smoothly and the quantity surveyor usually starts his work before all drawings are finished, and problems occur if amendments are made. The quantity surveyor, understandably, can become frustrated.

If your production information is not complete or not sufficiently complete for the quantity surveyor to commence an uninterrupted sequence of taking off, you have only two courses of action open to you:

❏ Send him what you have and follow up with the remainder of the information as quickly as possible in the hope that you can somehow 'keep him going'
❏ Inform him, as far in advance as possible, that you will not be able to deliver sufficient information by the appointed date and state a new date by which sufficient information can be ready

The first course, even if the quantity surveyor co-operates to the fullest, is the recipe for disaster because you will be bombarded with queries to such an extent that you will be unable to make adequate progress on the production information still outstanding. It is likely that the bills of quantities will be delayed and, more seriously, mistakes will occur.

If you set back the date one or two weeks, you will lose little; the quantity surveyor may even be able to recover some of the delay. The chances of mistakes will be reduced and your relationship will not be soured before the contract begins. Indeed, he may feel heartened by your readiness to state that you are not ready and your confident naming of a new date.

G2 Bills of quantities, if behind programme (39), (40)

You may find that, although you have co-ordinated all necessary information and delivered it to the quantity surveyor in good time, he falls behind the programme. He may notify you that the date for completion of the bills of quantities ready for sending out to tender must be put back.

Obviously, any delay tends to increase the tender sums. At some point during this stage you will have confirmed the list of tenderers and given them an indication of the date they can expect to receive the tender documents. In turn, they will have programmed the complex and expensive tendering process into their other work. Clearly, a delay can cause disruption to some contractors, depending upon the amount of work they have on their books. It may even mean that one or two contractors have to withdraw.

The sooner the quantity surveyor informs you that he cannot meet the date the better, so that you can notify the contractors **(39)** and, if necessary, choose new firms to replace any who withdraw. It is no use berating the quantity surveyor at this stage. The best laid plans go astray. It does no harm, however, to let him know that you will expect his help in keeping the cost down **(40)**.

39 Letter from architect to all contractors on tender list if quantity surveyor behind programme

Dear Sir

[*insert appropriate heading*]

I refer to my letter of [*insert date*] informing you that you had been included on the tender list of the above project and advising you of the provisional date when you could expect to receive the tender documents.

Unforeseen circumstances have caused a reassessment of that date and I expect to despatch the documents on [*insert date*].

Please check your programme of work and confirm, by return if possible, that you still wish and will be able to submit a tender in accordance with the revised dates.

Yours faithfully

Copy: Quantity surveyor

40 Letter from architect to quantity surveyor if behind programme

Dear Sir

[*insert appropriate heading*]

Thank you for your letter of [*insert date*] from which I note that you do not expect to be in a position to finalise the bills of quantities until [*insert date*]. This will be [*insert number*] weeks after the programmed date. It is unfortunate but we will have to make the best of it if there is no possibility of any improvement.

I have informed all the firms on the tender list that the tender documents will be delayed by approximately [*insert number*] weeks. Some firms may find themselves unable to tender because of other commitments and, in any case, the result may be a generally higher set of tenders. I do not think it is practicable or wise to try to cut down the tender period.

I know that you feel a certain responsibility for the situation but, equally, I know that I can rely upon you to help in negotiating a reduction in the lowest tender if it should prove necessary.

Yours faithfully

H Tender Action

H1 Client, if he wishes to accept the lowest, but unsatisfactory, tender (41)

It is normal good practice to open all tenders in the presence of your client. If there are no irregularities, usually the lowest tender is approved for acceptance.

It is assumed that the *Code of Procedure for Single Stage Selective Tendering 1994* has been adopted. When contractors respond to an invitation to tender on this or any other basis, your client is undertaking to carry out the procedures correctly and failure to do so may result in a contractor seeking damages for breach of the agreement. Tender forms which are amended or qualified should be rejected if you have given the tenderer the opportunity to withdraw the qualification without amendment to his tender and he has failed to do so.

Difficulties arise if your client wishes to accept a qualified tender which is the lowest by a substantial margin. He may care little for the Code of Procedure and look purely at the economics. Indeed, the qualifications may be, in retrospect, quite sensible. He may even wish to open and consider a late tender. You should endeavour to dissuade him, but if you fail, be sure to put the point to him in writing.

Obviously your professional integrity is also at stake, but it may not be advisable to mention it at this stage. Stick to the points your client will appreciate. If your letter fails to make any impression, you must seriously consider whether you wish to continue to be associated with the project. You can inform your client of your professional position at that point. When he sees that you mean what you say, he may think again.

41 Letter from architect to client if he wishes to accept the lowest but irregular tender

Dear Sir

[*insert appropriate heading*]

Following the meeting today at which tenders were opened, I should confirm the points I made so that you can give them proper consideration.

1   All tenderers were informed that the tendering procedure would be in accordance with the Code for Single Stage Selective Tendering 1994. Each tenderer would understand the full implications and they have the legal right to expect that, having expended a considerable amount of time and money on preparing tenders, the Code should be strictly applied. Failure to do so may result in an action for damages by one or more of the unsuccessful contractors.

2   A tenderer who amends the tender form, adds qualifications or submits a late tender is clearly seeking to gain an unfair advantage. As you know, [*insert name of firm*] was unwilling to withdraw his qualifications without amendment to his tender figure. If all tenderers had been given carte blanche to qualify their tenders as they thought fit, any yardstick for judging one firm against another would have vanished.

3   All other considerations apart, the adoption of a widely recognised system of tendering has a beneficial effect upon the whole construction industry in keeping prices down.

My advice is, therefore, that the irregular tender submitted by [*insert name*] should be rejected and the next lowest tender be subjected to the usual checking procedure. If no problems are encountered, I would be prepared to negotiate with the assistance of the quantity surveyor to achieve a lower contract figure which could be accepted.

Please let me have your instructions as soon as possible.

Yours faithfully

Copy: Quantity surveyor

J Project Planning

J1 Clerk of works: letter of instruction (42)

When the clerk of works is appointed, it is imperative that he knows precisely what is expected of him. If you have worked with him before, the situation is obviously better than that when an unfamiliar clerk of works is employed. In either case you should send a brief letter of instruction before work commences on site. Most firms have evolved their own report form and it would be superfluous to illustrate yet another.

MW 80

There is no provision for a clerk of works in the conditions but you may have made provision in the specification, possibly in terms similar to clause 3.10 of IFC 84. If so, this section is applicable.

J2 Letter of intent: contractor (43)

The general remarks regarding a letter of intent to sub-contractor and supplier apply to any letter of intent to the main contractor.

The occasions when such a letter has to be written should be rare, but some organisations have such ponderous administrative systems that they require a letter to be given to get things moving while the formal contract is being prepared. A potential problem is that the necessary procedures to create a legally binding contract may be overlooked. It is far from unknown for this to happen. The greatest danger for your client is that the contractor can leave site and abandon the works at any time, leaving your client without a remedy. In this situation, the contractor would be entitled to payment on a *quantum meruit* basis. Great care must be taken not to create a binding contract at this stage. You wish the contractor to do enough so that the whole project is not unduly delayed. Whether the contractor is prepared to operate on this basis is another matter. Your letter will be so guarded that you must not be surprised if the contractor rejects it.

42 Letter from architect to clerk of works giving instructions

Dear Sir

[*insert appropriate heading*]

My client, [*insert name*], has confirmed your appointment as clerk of works for the above contract. I should be pleased if you would call at this office on [*insert date*] at [*insert time*] to be briefed on the project and to collect your copies of drawings, schedules, bills of quantities/specification, weekly report forms, site diary and pad of direction forms [*delete as applicable*].

The contractor is expected to take possession of the site on [*insert date*]. You will be expected to be present on site [*insert periods during which the clerk of works is expected to be present*]. Let me know at the end of the first week if proper accommodation is not provided for you as described in the bills of quantities/specification [*delete as applicable*].

Your duties will be as indicated in the conditions of contract clause 12/3.10/specification [*delete as applicable*], a copy of which is enclosed for your reference. I wish to draw your attention to the following:

1 You will be expected to inspect all workmanship and materials to ensure conformity with the contract, i.e. the drawings, schedules, bills of quantities/specification [*delete as applicable*] and any further information and instructions issued from this office. Any defects must be pointed out to the person-in-charge, to whom you should address all comments. If any defects are left unremedied for twenty-four hours or if they are of a major or fundamental nature, you must let me know immediately by telephone.

2 The contract does not empower you to mark defective work on site although I am aware that it is common practice. You must not in any way deface materials on site whether or not they are incorporated into the structure.

3 It is not my policy to issue lists of defects to the contractor before practical completion. Commonly called snagging lists, they may be misinterpreted and give rise to disputes. Any lists of defects required should be produced by the person-in-charge. Please confine your remarks to the contractor to oral comments.

42   *continued*

4   The architect is the only person empowered to issue instructions to the contractor.

5   Any queries, unless of a minor explanatory nature, should be referred to me for decision. You are not empowered to issue any instructions varying, adding or omitting work.

6   The report sheets must be filled in completely and a copy sent to me on Monday of each week. Pay particular attention to listing all visitors to site and commenting on work done in as much detail as possible.

7   The diary is provided for you to enter up your daily comments.

8   Remember that your weekly reports and site diary may be called in evidence should a dispute arise so you must bear this in mind when making your entries and refrain from comments of a personal nature and from the use of unnecessary or extreme epithets.

[Add the following item if appropriate:]

9   I intend to make you my authorised representative for the purpose of verifying daywork sheets and for that purpose alone. Do not sign any sheets submitted later than the end of the week following the week in which work has been carried out nor any sheets with which you do not agree.

The successful completion of the contract depends in large measure upon your relationship with the contractor. If you are in any doubt upon anything please let me know.

Yours faithfully

43 Letter from architect to contractor: letter of intent

Dear Sir

[*insert appropriate heading*]

My client [*insert name*], has instructed me to inform you that your tender of [*insert date*] in the sum of [*insert amount in figures and words*] for the above project is acceptable and that I intend to prepare the main contract documents for signature subject to my client [*insert the provisos appropriate to the particular situation*].

It is not my client's intention that this letter, taken alone or in conjunction with your tender, should form a binding contract. However, my client is prepared to instruct you to [*insert the limited nature of the work required*].

If, for any reason whatsoever, the project does not proceed, my client's commitment will be strictly limited to payment for [*insert the limited nature of the work required*]. No other work included in your tender must be carried out without a further written order. No further obligation is placed upon my client and no obligation whatever, under any circumstances, is placed upon me.

Yours faithfully

J3 Consents: not received from planning authority (44), building control (45), (46), statutory undertakings (47)

If you discover, at this stage, that you have not obtained one of the necessary consents, your position is awkward. You will wish to avoid a delay which could cost your client money and which he will look to recover – probably from you. Even worse, if a consent is now refused, major redesign and retendering could result. It is convenient to deal with the major consents one at a time.

Planning authority

The reasons for not obtaining a consent are basically:

❑ You have not applied for one
❑ You have applied but a problem has delayed receipt

If you have not applied, clearly you must apply immediately. Two months are allowed for a decision unless the planning authority agreed with you to extend the time for making a decision. If you do not agree to an extension, the planning authority will make a decision on the application as it stands at that time. Failure to make a decision does not imply anything although you can appeal.

Simple applications are often decided well within the two months period. You will be conscious of:

❑ The period the lowest tender remains open for acceptance (usually three months)
❑ The attitude likely to be adopted by your client
❑ Any aspects of your scheme likely to be considered contentious by the planning authority

You should present your application personally and explain the situation to the planning officer – the chief planning officer himself if possible. Make absolutely sure that your project is going to be recommended for approval. This may take time because, if the scheme is any size at all, the planning authority will carry out extensive consultations with a large number of other authorities and they may require revisions. Do not attempt to commence work on site until approval has been obtained. The legal consequences can be dire and, in any case, you will not endear yourself to the planning authority.

Although the planning authority has to go through all the proper motions in considering an application, they will usually try their best to

44 Letter from architect to client if planning consent not obtained

Dear Sir

[*insert appropriate heading*]

[*First sentence optional depending on circumstances.*]

Checks on the lowest tender have been carried out and it has been found to be acceptable.

In carrying out my own checks prior to arranging a start on site, I note that planning consent has not been received. Work on site cannot commence before approval has been given. The lowest tender remains open for acceptance until [*insert date*] and, therefore, I do not propose to notify your acceptance to the contractor until I have planning approval.

I am pressing the planning authority to give approval as soon as possible.

Yours faithfully

45 Letter from architect to building control if application late

Dear Sir

[*insert appropriate heading*]

I refer to the meeting with your [*insert name*] on [*insert date*] when I deposited all the required documents to support an application for approval under the building regulations. I understand that the information supplied is likely to be satisfactory subject to your detailed checking.

Work on site is scheduled to commence on [*insert date*]. I trust that formal approval will be notified very shortly thereafter, but until it is received my client understands that he will be proceeding on site at his own risk.

Yours faithfully

Copy: Client

46 Letter from architect to client if building regulations approval not obtained

Dear Sir

[*insert appropriate heading*]

Approval under the building regulations has not yet been obtained for the above project. A start may be made on site at your own risk, i.e. if any work is found to be not in accordance with the building regulations, it would have to be corrected. I am as confident as it is reasonable to be that all the drawings conform with the regulations. Alternatively, the lowest tender need not be accepted until [*insert date*] and you may wish to wait. Approval will take up to five weeks.

Please let me have your instructions.

Yours faithfully

47 Letter from architect to statutory undertaking if late in requesting entry details

Dear Sir

[*insert appropriate heading*]

I refer to my visit to your office on [*insert date*] when I discussed the service requirements for the above project with your Mr [*insert name*].

I understand that you anticipate no difficulties in servicing and carrying out your work to conform with the main contractor's programme. I will ask him to contact you as soon as he is appointed.

I confirm that work is expected to commence on site on [*insert date*] and I understand that you will return my drawings with your services indicated thereon within the next few days.

Yours faithfully

speed things up as much as possible provided you play fair with them. You should also notify your client. (See letter **44**.)

If you have made application already and you have not yet received approval, telephone the planning authority immediately and explain your difficulty. There will be a reason why you have not received approval and it is essential that you sort out the problem without delay. How long it will take to receive approval will then depend on the authority. You will be tempted to stall for time. Unless you are sure that approval is to be given within days, stalling is bad policy as far as your client is concerned. He is entitled to know that the contract may be delayed.

Your letter may not satisfy your client but, although he may consider you careless (at the least), you have carried out your duty as soon as the situation became clear to you. You have not attempted to hide the facts and he should appreciate that. If he does not, he should be made to appreciate it by means of a personal meeting. You have made a serious mistake but you are not covering up and possibly making matters worse.

Building control

The reasons for not receiving building regulations approval are the same as for planning approval.

If you have not applied, do so immediately. Take the documents along personally and go through them with the building control officer to make sure that they are in order. There is a mandatory requirement to make an application by way of notice. This may be in the form of 'full plans', 'building notice', or 'initial notice' submitted by an approved inspector.

It is usual practice in such circumstances for building control to write stating that your client may proceed at his own risk pending approval of your application. Let your client know the position **(46)**.

Of course you must be sure that your building does conform to the regulations in every respect before you send such a letter. If you have already communicated acceptance to the lowest tenderer, you must adjust the letter accordingly and then you have little alternative but to proceed on site.

If you have already made application you should receive a decision within five weeks unless the authority obtains your permission to extend the period. If you do not receive a decision or a request to extend the time, the local authority is in breach of its duty and must refund the fee. There is no deemed approval. The operative date will have been notified to you immediately after your application has been received. If the authority request an extension, it will be for your benefit since it implies that your application is not acceptable in its present state. If you refuse an extension, the application will be refused.

Statutory undertakings (47)

The various statutory undertakings, principally gas, water and electricity suppliers, should have been consulted early in the project. They have certain obligations to supply services subject to the distance of your project from the mains. Any serious problems are likely to be encountered:

❏ In an entry to the building
❏ If you require a diversion of the existing mains or services

The requirements for service entry to buildings are generally well known and it is unusual for difficulties to arise if you have sent copies of your drawings to the appropriate suppliers so that they can indicate any special requirements. If you have forgotten to do that, take your drawings along by hand, discuss your service requirements and then confirm in writing.

A proposed diversion should be sorted out with the appropriate supplier at the earliest possible moment. If you have forgotten to do that, you should contact the supplier and discuss the problem. Assuming that a diversion is possible, the biggest difficulty is likely to be the cost. Statutory undertakings are normally prepared to give an estimate but nothing approaching a firm price. You will not know until after the work of each supplier is complete, including any diversions, what the final price will be. Therefore, there appears to be no good reason to worry your client with a report of the estimated cost of a late diversion unless it is likely to be very large.

K Operations on Site

K1 Commencement before formal contract (48), (49)

A frequent source of difficulty is the fact that the contractor wishes to start on site before the formal contract has been signed. Sometimes it is the employer who is anxious for the work to proceed as quickly as possible. If the contract documents are signed within a few days of the contractor taking possession of the site, it is doubtful whether there will be any side effects. However, if signing is delayed for several weeks, the contractor and the employer may find themselves asking the following questions:

❏ Is there any problem with regard to certification of monies due?
❏ Can *any* of the provisions of the formal contract be put into effect?
❏ What is the position if the employer or contractor decides to bring the project to an end after possession of the site but before signing?

The answers to all these questions will depend on:

❏ Whether a contract exists
❏ Whether a contract exists which incorporates the terms of the formal documents

The contractor will have been chosen usually from a group of tenderers, either because his price is lowest or for some other good reason. He will have tendered on the basis of bills of quantities, schedules of work, or specification and drawings. Since a contract is made by an offer, acceptance and consideration, everything depends upon the wording of the letter of acceptance from the employer (or from the architect on the employer's behalf) to the contractor (48).

This letter will form a valid binding contract leaving no room for doubt, and there is no difficulty in applying the provisions of the formal contract because they will have been referred to in the bills of quantities, schedules of work, or specification which form part of the basis of the contractor's tender. It follows, therefore, that neither side

48 Letter from architect to contractor accepting tender (correct version)

Dear Sir

[*insert appropriate heading*]

My client, [*insert name*], has instructed me to inform you that he accepts your tender dated [*insert date*] in the sum of [*insert sum in words*] for the above work in accordance with drawings numbered [*insert numbers*] and the bills of quantities, schedules of work, specification [*delete as applicable*].

In response to your request, my client informs me that he will allow you to take possession of the site on [*insert date*] and, consequently, the date for completion will be [*insert date*].

The contract documents are being prepared on this basis and will be forwarded to you for signature as soon as possible.

Yours faithfully

49 Letter from architect to contractor accepting tender (incorrect version)

Dear Sir

[*insert appropriate heading*]

My client, [*insert name*], has instructed me to inform you that he accepts your tender dated [*insert date*] in the sum of [*insert sum in words*] for the above work in accordance with the drawings numbered [*insert numbers*] and the bills of quantities/schedule of work/specification [*delete as appropriate*] subject to the agreement and signing of the formal contract documents. They will be forwarded to you as soon as possible for your agreement and signature.

In response to your request, my client instructs me that he will allow you to take possession of the site on [*insert date*] and, consequently, the date for completion will be [*insert date*].

Yours faithfully

can put an end to the contract without severe legal repercussions. Contrast letter **49**.

It is extremely doubtful whether letter **49** will complete a valid binding contract because it is an acceptance subject to further agreement. Generally, if the words 'subject to' appear in such a letter the result is that there is no contract incorporating the terms of the formal documents until the further agreement has been made and no provisions of the formal contract can be put into effect. It is possible that there is a contract of some kind based on conduct, but the terms are doubtful and certainly not those of the formal contract documents which are expressly excluded until the agreement and signing takes place. If, following the letter, the contractor begins work, but the formal documents are not agreed or signed, the amount payable to the contractor is uncertain and there are no terms covering, for example, extensions of time, loss and/or expense or determination. Alternatively, there may be no contract at all and the contractor may be entitled to a reasonable sum for work done. In such a situation, either party may simply bring the work to an end without serious penalty. The precise position depends upon the particular facts. The golden rule is never to allow a start on site before the formal documents are signed unless a very clear letter of acceptance is sent.

K2 Contract documents: initials missing (50)

Deletions or additions to the conditions should be initialled by both parties, preferably at the beginning and end of each such amendment.

More often than one cares to admit, a set of initials is missed. Experience shows that this most often occurs as a mistake by the employer.

If the amendment is clearly the intention of the parties as evidenced by the bills of quantities, schedules of work, or specification, it is probably best to let the matter lie provided that it does not attempt to override or modify the printed conditions. Clause 2.2.1 of JCT 80, clause 1.3 of IFC 84 and clause 4.1 of MW 80 expressly prevent such overriding or modification. If the amendment is evidenced in the bills, schedules or specification, but conflicts with the printed conditions or if it is the result of negotiation (perhaps oral) before acceptance of the tender the matter is more serious. It is then vital that the amendment is initialled as evidence of what the parties intend.

What the parties intended at the beginning is often, as we all know, different from what they wish they had intended later in the contract. In that case it is better to get the difficulty sorted out earlier rather than later.

50 Letter from architect to client or contractor (depending on whose initials are missing) to initial an amendment

Dear Sir

[*insert appropriate heading*]

It has been drawn to my attention that you have omitted to initial one of the agreed amendments to the conditions of contract. In order to rectify the matter it would be appreciated if you would ask your [*insert name of the person who originally signed the document*] to telephone me to arrange a mutually suitable time to correct the omission.

Yours faithfully

Note that it is inadvisable to specify the precise amendment because the result might be that Mr (whoever originally signed) will give the matter considerable thought and decide that the amendment was ill-judged. On the other hand, if he is simply presented with the document to initial, it is more than likely he will recognise the amendment as one to which he agreed and initial it accordingly. There is nothing wrong or devious in doing things this way since you are only concerned with correcting a clear oversight, but doing it in a way which recognises the vagaries of human nature.

K3 Contract documents: drawings amended (51), (52)

When the contract drawings have been prepared for sending out to tender, it is essential to take off spare copies of each one so that they will be available for inclusion in the contract documents. Some firms employ the sensible practice of producing copy negatives from each contract drawing so that there is no chance of a mistake if extra copies are required. If computer aided draughting is used, a tape containing the appropriate data must be set on one side.

If one of these procedures is not adopted, it is probable that the original negatives will have undergone some revision before the formal contract is signed. You will be faced with the task of altering the drawings back to their original state before incorporating them in the formal contract. Some confusion is certain to result. It is crucial that the drawings with the invitation to tender and the drawings in the formal contract are identical otherwise dispute will almost certainly result. If you forget, there is no real alternative but to alter the drawings as soon as you discover your mistake and invite both contractor and client to sign them again. It is best that no time is wasted so do not simply send the drawings or ask the client or contractor to call around to your office sometime. Recognise that it is your fault and be prepared to take some trouble to put matters right.

K4 Drawings, schedules: not ready (53), (54)

It is your responsibility to ensure that the contractor has two copies of 'any descriptive schedules or other like documents necessary for use in carrying out the works' (clause 5.3.1.1) and you must provide them 'so soon as is possible' (clause 5.3.1). It is not uncommon for the architect to be behind in the production of detailed drawings. In this situation

51 Letter from architect to contractor inviting him to re-sign new contract drawings

Dear Sir

[*insert appropriate heading*]

On perusal of the signed contract drawings, it is clear that numbers [*insert numbers of defective drawings*] do not correspond precisely with the drawings on which you tendered because later amendments were incorporated.

In order to ensure a proper record of the contract, I have prepared a new set of drawings, altered back to their original state, and propose calling on you at [*insert time*] on [*insert date*] so that you can satisfy yourself that the new set are identical with those on which you tendered, and sign them. I will bring a spare set for your retention. Please let me know if the time suggested is convenient.

Yours faithfully

52   Letter from architect to client inviting him to re-sign new contract drawings

Dear Sir

[*insert appropriate heading*]

On perusal of the signed contract drawings, it is clear that numbers [*insert numbers of defective drawings*] do not correspond precisely with the drawings on which the contractor tendered because later amendments were incorporated.

In order to ensure a proper record of the contract, I have prepared a new set of drawings altered back to their original state and propose calling on you at [*insert time*] on [*insert date*] so that you can add your signature to that of the contractor which I have already obtained. Please let me know if the time suggested is inconvenient.

Yours faithfully

53 Letter from architect to contractor if all drawings are not available

Dear Sir

[*insert appropriate heading*]

Thank you for your letter of [*insert date*].

If you wish to persist in your claim perhaps you will let me have full supporting information.

Quite frankly, however, I think that you are premature. I confirm that, in my opinion, you have all the information reasonably necessary for you to proceed with the works.

Having said that, I do welcome any selective requests for specific information made in good time. Such a procedure is of mutual benefit. I will be sending you further details from time to time but do please let me know if there is any particular drawing you require within the next week.

Yours faithfully

54 Letter from architect to contractor if important drawings not available

Dear Sir

[*insert appropriate heading*]

Thank you for your letter of [*insert date*].

Will you let me have full evidence in support of your claim as soon as possible.

It is not usual, as you know, to supply every single detail at the commencement of the contract. However, if you will let me have precise information regarding the drawings and schedules you need immediately, including why you need them at this stage, I will ensure that they are sent to you.

Yours faithfully

the contractor sometimes tries to gain advantage by making application for all the drawings to be delivered to him immediately the contract is signed. The contractor often threatens unspecified claims for extension of time and loss and/or expense.

Fortunately, a number of other clauses in the contract clarify the position. Clause 5.4 modifies 5.3.1.1 by placing a duty on you to issue further drawings or details 'as and when from time to time may be necessary'. Clauses 25.4.6 and 26.2.1 make reference to the drawings and details being requested by the contractor on a date that is not unreasonably distant from the date on which it is necessary for him to receive them if he is to be entitled to extension of time or loss and/or expense. A sufficiently annotated and updated programme could satisfy this obligation.

Of course, every contractor would like to have all the information he needs to build right at the beginning of the job. The contract, however, provides for the realities. Most contractors appreciate the fact. Some, as noted earlier, will try to make capital out of the situation.

The first thing for you to do is to check that the contractor has got everything he immediately needs for building or ordering purposes. It is to some extent a subjective test which you must try to carry out as fairly as possible. Assuming that you are happy that the contractor has all the drawings he reasonably requires, you should answer the contractor's claims **(53)**.

IFC 84

The position is somewhat different. The conditions do not specify when you must let the contractor have 'further drawings or details'. However you are obliged to provide them as reasonably necessary to enable the contractor to carry out and complete the works in accordance with the contract. Reference to extension of time and loss and/or expense for late delivery of information is contained in clauses 2.4.7 and 4.12.1 respectively.

MW 80

The situation is similar to IFC 84. Note also, that there is no reference to claims for loss and/or expense other than in a limited way as a result of carrying out architects' instructions requiring variations, but that does not mean that the contractor will not make any. Any such claims would have to be referred to the employer for his decision. The letter should serve four purposes:

- ❏ It should show your willingness to examine any properly presented claim
- ❏ It should gently let the contractor know that his current claim is recognised as a device only
- ❏ It should confirm that all necessary drawings have been handed over
- ❏ It should indicate the desire to co-operate in a logical sequence of information provision. It is always best to agree a series of dates with the contractor so that drawings can be supplied at the right time.

The problem really occurs if the contractor is correct and he does not have all the information he needs. You will have a good idea what is missing and, no doubt, all available staff will be working on the project. You can either admit that the information is not ready and brace yourself for the inevitable claim or you can attempt to defuse the situation and buy a little time **(54)**.

In order to substantiate a claim that he has not received all necessary drawings at the beginning of the contract, it will be necessary for the contractor to indicate the drawings required and state why he needs each one. That is a formidable task. Rather than expend time and energy producing such a claim which would be the subject of much argument, he may opt for the easy way out by simply naming his priority drawings. Do not forget that he does not wish to jeopardise relations on the whole contract at the very beginning if matters can be settled quickly so that he can get on with his job. Presumably that is your view also.

K5 Failure to give possession on the due date (55)

If the employer fails to give possession on the date noted in the appendix, the difficulty can usually be remedied by the employer deferring the giving of possession provided the appropriate clause (23.1.2) is stated in the appendix to apply. The deferment period must not exceed six weeks or whatever lesser period is stated in the appendix. Clearly, the earlier the employer can notify the contractor the better. Deferment will entitle the contractor to an extension of time under clause 25.4.13; indeed you must grant such extension if the employer is not to lose his right to deduct liquidated damages for the contractor's own delays. Deferment will also entitle the contractor to make application for reimbursement of loss and/or expense under clause 26.1 and, therefore, the greater the notice which can be given, the easier it is for

55 Letter from architect to contractor if possession not given on due date and no deferment provision

Dear Sir

[*insert appropriate heading*]

I have been informed by my client that he will be unable to give you possession of the site/whole site [*delete as appropriate*] on the due date.

However, he assures me that possession will be given on [*insert date*]. I have suggested to him that both the date for commencement[1] and the date for completion should be set back by [*insert number of days related to delay in possession*] days and that the contract should be amended accordingly. If you agree with this course of action, I should be pleased if you would let me know as soon as possible.

Yours faithfully

Copy: Employer

---

[1]   *Substitute 'possession' when using JCT 80 or IFC 84*

the contractor to mitigate any losses. If is, of course, possible to amend the deferment period in the appendix and also clause 23.1.2 to allow a period in excess of six weeks, but no doubt an increased period would be reflected in the tender price as inserting a large element of uncertainty into any programme. If the deferment clause is not stated to apply, there is a serious breach of contract as described under MW 80 below.

IFC 84

The position under this contract is broadly similar. It should be noted, however, that the period of deferment is stated as not exceeding the period stated in the appendix which should not exceed six weeks. The clauses under which you should grant an extension of time and under which the contractor may make application for reimbursement of loss and/or expense are 2.4.14 and 4.11 (a) respectively. If the deferment clause is not stated to apply, there is a serious breach of contract as described under MW 80 below.

MW 80

The position is very serious under this form of contract. It is a serious breach and the contractor can determine his employment under clause 7.3.1.2 or, under certain circumstances, treat it as repudiation at common law, bring the contract to an end and recover substantial damages. You must do two things:

❏ Try to ensure possession of the site within seven days of the commencement date.
❏ Try to get the contractor to agree in writing to putting back the commencement and completion dates by seven days. This amounts to varying the contract terms which requires the employer's authority. If the contractor agrees, you should ensure that both parties amend, and initial, the printed conditions accordingly. He may also wish to claim some damages but that must be preferable to allowing him to determine. Each case must be judged on its merits **(55)**.

Immediately inform your client of the situation by telephone. If you cannot secure possession within seven days and the contractor will not agree to an extension of time, your client will have to face the consequences of his own action or inaction.

K6 Meetings: standing of minutes as a record (56), (57)

Minutes are often referred to by the contractor or architect in claims for extension of time or loss and/or expense. Provided that there is a proper record at each meeting that the minutes of the previous meeting are agreed by all parties, the minutes will stand as a true record of the matters contained therein.

Lack of recorded agreement reduces their standing and value considerably to that of a mere note produced by one side only. This is not to say they have no value. They may well be of crucial importance particularly if there is no evidence to the contrary.

Where the contract requires the issue of a certificate of any kind, written notice or instruction, you should not attempt to issue them as minutes. Their standing would be, at best, doubtful.

You should make it clear that you will chair your contract meetings and produce the minutes. It will enable you to ensure that all items discussed are recorded to your satisfaction.

If the contractor chairs the meeting or if he sends you minutes of other meetings which he has held, you must check them carefully for errors and implications. Write immediately if there is anything with which you disagree. Do not wait until the next meeting. If the contractor sends you his own version of your meeting, you should return it with an appropriate response **(57)**.

K7 Master programme: alleged approval by architect (58), (59), (60)

The 1980 Form of Contract is the first JCT contract to make any reference to the contractor's master programme. It requires the contractor to supply two copies to the architect and update it within 14 days of any revision of the completion date by the architect. In doing so, it simply states in the printed conditions what has long been present in most contracts through an appropriate clause in the bills of quantities, schedule of work or specification. It is still possible to delete the provision, of course – a possibility emphasised by the footnote, although not one which any architect should seriously consider. Although the contract conditions do not state the form the programme should take, it is usual for the architect to specify the type of programme he requires in the bills of quantities, schedules of work or specification, e.g. bar chart, network analysis, precedence diagram etc.

56   Letter from architect to contractor regarding items in minutes of meeting

Dear Sir

[*insert appropriate heading*]

I have examined the minutes of the meeting held on site on [*insert date*] which I received today. I have the following comments to make:

[*insert list of comments*]

Please arrange to have these comments published at the next meeting and inserted in the appropriate place in the minutes.

Yours faithfully

Copies: to all those present at the meeting and included in the original circulation

57 Letter from architect to contractor if contractor sends his own version of meeting

Dear Sir

[*insert appropriate heading*]

Thank you for your letter of [*insert date*] with which you enclosed what appear to be your own notes of the meeting held on [*insert date*].

There appears to be a misunderstanding. The position is that I will chair and produce minutes for all meetings which I call in connection with this contract. If there is anything with which you disagree, it should be raised at the next meeting or by letter to me as appropriate. By now, you will have received the minutes of the above meeting. Your own notes are, therefore, returned with this letter.

Yours faithfully

58 Letter from architect to contractor referring to the master programme

Dear Sir

[*insert appropriate heading*]

Thank you for your letter of [*insert date*] with which you enclosed two copies of your master programme.

I have the following points to make:

[*Insert a list of all the points on which you are doubtful. It is best to write them in the form of questions, e.g. are you satisfied that you have allowed sufficient time to complete the central heating, bearing in mind the other internal works you propose to carry out at the same time?*]

I have no further comments to make at this time, but you must not take any lack of comment to indicate approval to the programme in part or in whole. The organisation and method of working and the time allocated to particular activities is your responsibility to carry out within the constraints laid down by the drawings and bills of quantities/schedules of work/ specification [*delete as applicable*].

Your master programme is received as an indication of your intentions only. The use of the programme as evidence in any future consideration of extension of time or loss and/or expense is a matter for my discretion.

Yours faithfully

59 Letter from architect to contractor refuting approval if approval not given to the master programme

Dear Sir

[*insert appropriate heading*]

Thank you for your letter of [*insert date*] to which I will reply in detail in due course.

Before I do so, however, I must put on record that I have never given approval to your master programme in part or in whole. Indeed, it would have been quite inappropriate for me to do so because the responsibility for carrying out the work, including method and time, is yours, subject only to the constraints laid down in the drawings and bills of quantities/ schedules of work/specification[*delete as appropriate*].

That is not to say, of course, that I will not take your programme into consideration in arriving at my decision. It is a matter for my discretion.

Yours faithfully

60 Letter from architect to contractor qualifying approval if approval already given to the master programme

Dear Sir

[*insert appropriate heading*]

Thank you for your letter of [*insert date*] to which I will reply in detail in due course.

Before I do so, however, I should clarify the situation in respect of the approval to the master programme you allege was given in my letter of [*insert date*].

[*Omit the following paragraph if IFC 84 or MW 80 used.*]

Clause 5.3.2 provides that no obligations are imposed upon the parties by the master programme beyond those imposed by the contract documents.

Clearly, my expressed approval was given in the sense that I could see no objection to the way in which you proposed to carry out the work nor to the time you allocated to the project. It cannot remove your responsibility for ensuring that the work is carried out in accordance with the contract.

Yours faithfully

The provision of a programme is particularly important for the purpose of:

❏ Accurately monitoring the contractor's actual compared to his proposed progress
❏ Estimating a fair and reasonable extension of time
❏ Deciding upon the validity of a claim for prolongation costs

For these purposes, a precedence diagram or network analysis is invaluable.

Depending upon the precise facts, the status of the contractor's programme may not be absolutely clear. Provided it is not signed and bound in with the contract documents nor accepted as part of the contractor's tender, it is not a contract document. If, however, it can be shown that you have approved the programme it is persuasive evidence that you considered the time periods and, perhaps, dates for receipt of information to be reasonable.

The contractor will often allege that the architect has approved the programme, in order perhaps to bolster his claim for an extension of time which depends upon failure to achieve some programmed dates. The allegation is more difficult to refute if the bills of quantities, schedules of work or specification require the contractor to submit a programme 'for the approval of the architect'. Approval of the programme may not be significant, but it is best not to put it to the test.

When you receive the programme, you will certainly make some comment if it does not appear to correspond with the contract period. If you have required the programme to be submitted for your approval, it may seem reasonable that if you do not object, you approve, although the better view is that in such cases approval must be expressed and cannot be presumed by silence. In any event, you should take great care when you receive the master programme **(58)**.

IFC 84 and MW 80

There is no reference to a master programme in the conditions, but it is still possible to require one in the specification and in such a case the above remarks and the letters are applicable.

If you did not write this kind of letter, making your respective positions perfectly clear, the contractor may, usually at a much later date, in the process of a claim, allege your approval. There are two possible letters in reply. One, if you have never actually stated that you approved his programme, another if you have been unwise enough to indicate approval in writing **(59)**, **(60)**.

K8 Printed conditions and bills of quantities (or specification) not agreed in agreement (61)

Over-zealousness or lack of communication between architect and quantity surveyor can lead to contradictions occurring between the printed conditions and the bills of quantities, schedules of work or specification. The areas in which such differences can occur are limitless, but a simple example would be where the bills of quantities attempt to extend the architect's power to give instructions beyond the limits clearly defined by the conditions.

Sometimes the contractor seeks to rely on the provisions in the bills of quantities or specification, but more often it is the employer, through his representative, the architect.

Clause 2.2.1 of the conditions states: 'Nothing contained in the contract bills shall override or modify the application or interpretation of that which is contained in the articles of agreement, the conditions or the appendix'.

(Clauses 1.3 of IFC 84 and 4.1 of MW 80 are to much the same effect although variously referring to contract drawings, specifications, schedules or schedules of work.)

Although the general law is that type (or handwriting) prevails over print, it is now established that clause 2.2.1 is effective to reverse that rule so far as JCT 80 and similar contracts are concerned.

Note that the clause only comes into effect if the bills of quantities etc, seek to 'override or modify' so that the bills of quantities etc, can contain instructions for the work to be done in a particular sequence or introduce other matters which will be binding provided they do not attempt to override or modify.

Assuming that you have received a challenge from the contractor on the grounds that the conditions say something different from what is contained in the bills of quantities (or specification) you must concede **(61)**.

K9 Contractor not prepared to correct a perceived deficiency in his statement (62)

There may be certain parts of the building, such as perhaps a suspended concrete floor, which you have identified in the appendix to the contract and on the contract drawings and in the bills of quantities (specification) as 'performance specified work'. The contractor must provide a contractor's statement showing how he intends to satisfy the

61 Letter from architect to contractor referring to conflict between conditions and bills of quantities (or specification)

Dear Sir

[*insert appropriate heading*]

Thank you for your letter of [*insert date*].

The point you raise is valid.

[*That is all you need to say; the less said the better. Depending upon the point at issue, however, you may be able to add a paragraph attacking the situation from another angle such as:*]

I would, however, draw your attention to clause [*insert clause number*] which deals with the matter in dispute.

Yours faithfully

62 Letter from architect to contractor if refusal to correct deficiency

This letter is not suitable for use with IFC 84 or MW 80

Dear Sirs

[*insert appropriate heading*]

Thank you for your letter of the [*insert date*].

I note with concern that you refuse to correct the deficiency in your contractor's statement, apparently because the contract does not expressly require you to do so after receipt of my clause 42.6 notice.

Take this as notice that if you proceed to construct the [*describe the work*] without correcting the deficiency, I shall immediately use my powers under clause 8.4.1 to instruct removal from site followed by further instructions under clause 8.4.3 requiring variations as a consequence. I draw to your attention that such variations will not result in any increase in the contract sum nor any extension of time or payment of loss and/or expense.

I suggest that you reconsider your decision and correct the deficiency as requested.

Yours faithfully

employer's requirements and you may consider that it is deficient in certain respects. The position is clear and clause 42.6 places a duty on you to inform the contractor of the shortcoming. There is no stipulation that you must do this in writing, but it is obviously sensible to do so. If the reason for the deficiency is because you did not correctly specify the requirements in the first place, it is not strictly a deficiency and you will have to issue an architect's instruction under clause 42.11 requiring a variation.

A problem may arise if your requirements were clear, the contractor's statement was deficient, but on receipt of your letter he refuses to make any changes, saying that he has satisfied the requirements. The contract gives no clear guidance about your next move. Probably, if the situation is sufficiently serious, you can simply issue an instruction omitting the work and adding back a design of your own to satisfy the requirements. That may well involve some delay and the contractor would make out a case for extension of time and perhaps loss and/or expense. You know it is all the contractor's fault, but proving it is another matter. If the contractor is allowed to proceed, it should become obvious whether he has satisfied the performance requirements. If the situation is not so serious, although in need of rectification, you could try putting him on notice **(62)**.

IFC 84 and MW 80

There is no provision for performance specified work under these forms of contract.

K10 Discrepancy between bills of quantities, schedules of work, numbered documents or specification or statutory requirements and contract documents, not found by the contractor (63)

It is now settled that your obligation is to provide the contractor with correct information. He has no obligation to check the drawings for discrepancies. Naturally, if he is carrying out his job properly, he should find discrepancies as he plans his work, but if they are not discovered until they have been constructed, it seems that you are in a very tough position.

The contractor also has to use proper skill and care, of course, and if you suspect that the real reason for failure to detect the discrepancy is

63 Letter from architect to contractor if discrepancy not discovered before construction

Dear Sir

I refer to [*insert appropriate heading*].

I find it difficult to understand how any contractor, let alone one of your undoubted experience, could have proceeded with the construction of [*briefly describe*]. There is, admittedly, a discrepancy between . . . and [*insert names of documents*], but it is just the kind of inconsistency which you could have been expected to discover as you were planning to carry out the work.

Before I can feel justified in seeking authorisation for further expenditure in this matter, I should be pleased if you would let me have a brief report setting down exactly how it was possible for you to reach this stage without finding the discrepancy. In the report, you should make reference to the precise documents you consulted before ordering and construction stages.

Yours faithfully

Copy: Quantity surveyor

carelessness or even malice, you should make the appropriate inquiries before you issue any instructions **(63)**.

K11 Certification, if claim not yet ascertained (64), (65), (66)

Clause 3 of the conditions of contract stipulates that if the contract sum is to be adjusted by an amount, then as soon as the amount is ascertained in whole or in part, it should be taken into account in the computation of the next interim certificate following the ascertainment.

Problems tend to arise because, understandably, the contractor will press for the implementation of clause 3 at the earliest possible moment, sometimes even going so far as to accuse you of being in breach of your duty under the contract. Apart from extra work, which is relatively easy to ascertain, the commonest areas for which the contractor seeks extra payment are claims for loss and/or expense and fluctuations. Claims for loss and/or expense will be dealt with later but the principle for your reply should be the same in each case.

❏ Where the contractor has not provided such details as are reasonably necessary for ascertainment to take place **(64)**
❏ Where the contractor has provided all details necessary, but ascertainment has not taken place **(65)**, **(66)**

Without doubt, the contractor will write or telephone you, demanding to know what further information you could possibly require. The best thing is to arrange for the quantity surveyor to write directly to him, giving a list of the information needed **(65)**.

IFC 84

Clauses 3.6–3.8 provide for variations and provisional sums and clauses 4.2 and 4.3 allow for adjustment of the certificates. Clauses 4.11 and 4.12 provide for the ascertainment of loss and/or expense.

MW 80

Clauses 3.6 and 3.7 provide for variations and provisional sums and clauses 4.2 and 4.3 allow for adjustment of the certificates. Letter **64** is applicable.

Provision is made for the appointment of a quantity surveyor but he is not referred to in the conditions. It is assumed that no quantity

64 Letter from architect to contractor if necessary details not provided

Dear Sir

[*insert appropriate heading*]

Thank you for your letter of [*insert date*].

I can understand your anxiety to receive all monies due to you as soon as possible. In order to achieve that end, you have a duty to provide all information reasonably necessary for the ascertainment to be carried out. You have not yet provided the information. As soon as you do so, the ascertainment will be carried out as quickly as practicable and the monies, if any, due will be included in the next certificate following such ascertainment.

Yours faithfully

Copy: Quantity surveyor

65 Letter from architect to quantity surveyor asking him to write to the contractor regarding ascertainment

This letter is not usually suitable for use with MW 80

Dear Sir

[*insert appropriate heading*]

I have received a telephone call from the main contractor/I have received a letter from the main contractor [*use the appropriate phrase*] dated [*insert date*], a copy of which is enclosed.

He is obviously anxious to get any money to which he may be entitled as soon as possible. He considers that he has sent all the information required for ascertainment.

Will you write to him please, and let him have a list of everything required before the process of ascertainment can proceed.

Naturally, I do not expect you to do any calculations until you are fully satisfied that you have all the information you need.

Yours faithfully

66   Letter from architect to contractor when information has been provided but ascertainment has not taken place

Dear Sir

[*insert appropriate heading*]

Thank you for your letter of [*insert date*].

You submitted/The quantity surveyor informs me that you submitted [*use appropriate phrase*] the last items of information necessary for the ascertainment on [*insert date*]. The quantity surveyor is proceeding with his[1] checking and calculations as quickly as possible. It is conceivable that, in the course of ascertainment, there may be one or two points which require clarification. In order to save as much time as possible, I am asking the quantity surveyor to write directly to you on such items.[2]

[*Add only if the contractor alleges that you are in breach:*]

I reject your suggestion that either the quantity surveyor or myself is[3] in breach. We are carrying out our[4] duties strictly in accordance with the contract and with complete fairness to you and the employer.

Yours faithfully

Copy: Quantity surveyor

---

[1]   *Substitute 'I am proceeding with my' when using MW 80*
[2]   *Omit underlined words when using MW 80*
[3]   *Substitute 'I am' when using MW 80*
[4]   *Substitute 'I am carrying out my' when using MW 80*

surveyor has been appointed and, therefore, letter **65** is not applicable.

K12 Certification: certificate not received by the employer (67)

Clause 5.8 provides that except where specifically so provided, any certificate to be issued by the architect shall be issued to the employer with a duplicate copy immediately to the contractor.

Clause 30.1.1.1 provides that the contractor should be entitled to payment within 14 days from the date of issue of each interim certificate.

Clause 5.8 applies to any certificate for any purpose which the architect may issue, but difficulties most often occur with financial certificates, for obvious reasons.

The issue of a certificate directly to an employer has two important results:

❏ It removes from the contractor the onus of presenting the certificate for payment
❏ It effectively reduces the length of time available to the employer for honouring certificates by the time elapsing between the issue of the certificate and receipt by the employer. Partly for this reason, it is common practice for the 14 day period to be amended to 21 or even 28 days.

It is obviously important that the employer receives the certificate at the earliest possible moment, particularly so in the case of a local authority or some other large public body where the issue of cheques follows a special procedure. You can adopt one of a number of measures to ensure that there are no hiccups at this vital stage (the contractor can commence steps to determine his employment under the contract if he is not paid on time, clause 28.2.1):

❏ Take the certificate to the employer by hand on the day of issue
❏ Send the certificate by registered post or recorded delivery
❏ Telephone the employer on the day of issue, informing him of the sums involved and send the certificate by first class post

Delivery by hand is the most satisfactory, if the distance is not too great, because it combines certainty with minimum delay. Remember to have a form of receipt ready for the employer to sign and date for your records.

The problem is that there will be many things that you do which are

67   Letter from architect to employer if certificate has not arrived on time

Dear Sir

[*insert appropriate heading*]

I refer to your telephone call today.

A copy of certificate number [*insert number*] is enclosed. It is essential that you take whatever steps are necessary to get a cheque for the full amount to the contractor immediately. It is inadvisable to assume that you have a full seven days to pay because, technically, the certificate is not discharged until your cheque has been cleared through the bank. I suggest that you arrange to have the cheque delivered by hand, but be sure to obtain a signed and dated receipt.

If you allow the contractor to determine his employment the consequences will be extensive extra cost and considerable delay to the project.

I issued the certificate on [*insert date*]. Why you have not received it is not known and is of academic interest only in the present circumstances. This is the first time that this problem has occurred but, in the future, all certificates will be sent to you by recorded delivery and I will arrange to telephone you within two days of the date of issue to check that you have received them.

Yours faithfully

of great importance, of which the issue of the certificate is but one. It is totally impractical to take everything to everybody by hand unless your organisation is large enough to employ a special messenger. It is all too easy to slip into the habit of sending certificates by first class post and assuming that they will arrive on the employer's desk the following day. Despite what is said about postal services, this method will work quite satisfactorily in the vast majority of cases. But your typist may make a mistake on the envelope or, for some other reason, the employer may not receive the certificate. The first intimation you are likely to receive is when the employer telephones you to say that he has received notice from the contractor giving him seven days to pay on threat of determination of employment under clause 28.1.1. What is your position and what should you do?

- ❑ You have already issued the certificate at the proper time (events show that the contractor must have received his copy) so you have fulfilled your duty. The employer, however, is unlikely to be impressed by your efficiency.
- ❑ Send a duplicate copy to the employer by hand – whatever the cost – together with a letter **(67)**.

IFC 84

The scheme of certificates is much the same as JCT 80 although simpler. Clause 1.9 provides that they are to be issued to the employer with a copy to the contractor. Clause 4.2 stipulates that payment is to be made within 14 days of the date of issue. The other remarks and letter **67** are applicable to this form also.

MW 80

It is not absolutely clear to whom the certificates should be issued. Clause 4.2 refers to the architect certifying 'progress payments to the contractor'. That clause can be interpreted in two ways:

- ❑ The architect is to certify progress payments due to the contractor
- ❑ The architect is to certify to the contractor the amount of progress payments

On balance it would appear, on the wording and since no other indication is given elsewhere in the conditions, that progress payments should be certified and the certificate issued to the employer, because it is the employer's duty to pay within 14 days of the date of the certificate. Naturally you will issue a copy to the contractor. Whichever method you adopt, the clause makes it clear that payment is due within

14 days of the date of the certificate, and clause 7.3.1.1 refers to 'amount properly due'. The obligation of the employer to pay within a particular period is established and, therefore, the bulk of the general remarks in this section except those specifically referring to clause numbers of the standard form apply. Letter **67** is appropriate also.

Fortunately, provided the employer acts promptly, ill effects can be avoided.

K13 Instruction: contractor's refusal to carry out forthwith (68), (69), (70), (71), (72), (Flowchart 1)

Clause 4.1.1 deals with the contractor's obligation to comply forthwith with all instructions issued by the architect in respect of matters on which he is expressly empowered by the conditions to issue instructions. There are two exceptions. Firstly variations within the meaning of clause 13.1.2, when the contractor need not comply to the extent that he makes reasonable objection to the architect in writing. Whether the objection is reasonable is something to be decided, first by the architect and ultimately, if there is a dispute, by an arbitrator. You would be advised to consider any objection by the contractor very carefully before deciding that it is not reasonable. Secondly, it is thought that, if the contractor, after requesting the architect to specify the clause empowering the instruction, decides to seek arbitration, he has the right to await the outcome before complying.

If the contractor receives a perfectly straightforward instruction and, far from carrying it out forthwith, appears to be taking no action whatever, you can send him a notice in accordance with clause 4.1.2 **(68)**.

IFC 84

Architect's instructions are dealt with by clause 3.5. It is similar to JCT 80 except that there is no provision for confirming oral instructions. Letters **68** to **72** inclusive, **Flowchart 1** and the other general remarks in this section are applicable.

MW 80

Clause 3.5 relates to architect's instructions. It is very brief and states that the architect may issue written instructions 'which the contractor shall forthwith carry out'. There is a provision for a seven days com-

68 Letter from architect to contractor giving notice requiring compliance with an instruction

REGISTERED POST/RECORDED DELIVERY [as appropriate]

Dear Sir

[insert appropriate heading]

Take this as notice under clause 4.1.2[1] of the conditions of contract that I require you to comply with my instruction number [insert number] dated [insert date], a further copy of which is enclosed.

If within seven days of receipt of this notice you have not complied, the employer may employ and pay other persons to execute any work whatsoever which may be necessary to give effect to the instruction. All costs incurred in connection with such employment will be deducted from money due or to become due to you under the contract or will be recovered from you as a debt.

Yours faithfully

Copies: Employer
Quantity surveyor

---

[1] *Substitute '3.5.1' when using IFC 84 and '3.5' when using MW 80*

69 Letter from architect to contractor if contractor fails to comply within seven days (date at least seven days from previous notice)

REGISTERED POST/RECORDED DELIVERY [*as appropriate*]

Dear Sir

[*insert appropriate heading*]

I refer to the notice issued to you on [*insert date*] in accordance with clause 4.1.2[1] referring to my instruction number [*insert number*] dated [*insert date*].

I confirm that I have inspected the works this morning and you have not complied with my instruction.

The employer is taking immediate steps to employ others to carry out the work. All costs in connection with such employment will be deducted from money due or to become due to you under the contract or will be recovered from you as a debt.

Yours faithfully

Copies: Employer
Quantity surveyor

[1] *Substitute '3.5.1' when using IFC 84 and '3.5' when using MW 80*

70 Letter from architect to contractor if he carries out instructions after another firm's quotation accepted

Dear Sir

[*insert appropriate heading*]

You were instructed to carry out the work contained in my instruction number [*insert number*] dated [*insert date*]. Clause 4.1.1[1] requires you to comply with instructions forthwith. This you failed to do.

In accordance with clause 4.1.2[1] I sent you a notice dated [*insert date*] requiring you to comply with my instruction within seven days. On [*insert date*] I notified you that you were in breach of your obligations under the contract and the work would be carried out by others. Subsequently, on [*insert date*], you carried out the instruction.

The employer has been subject to costs in connection with the employment of others and, in accordance with clause 4.1.2[1], those costs will be deducted from money due or to become due to you or will be recovered from you as a debt.

Yours faithfully

Copies: Employer
　　　　 Quantity surveyor

---

[1]   *Substitute '3.5.1' when using IFC 84 and '3.5' when using MW 80*

71 Letter from architect to contractor agreeing to a later date for carrying out instructions

Dear Sir

[*insert appropriate heading*]

Thank you for your letter of [*insert date*].

I note that you propose to complete the work detailed in my instruction number [*insert number*] dated [*insert date*] on [*insert date*].

After careful consideration, I am prepared to agree to your proposal on the understanding that the employer does not waive any of his rights and remedies under the contract. This means that if you default in completing the work on [*insert contractor's proposed date*] the notice sent to you on [*insert date*] will have expired and, without further notice, the employer will employ others to carry out the work.

Yours faithfully

Copies: Employer
Quantity surveyor

72 Letter from architect to contractor not agreeing to a later date for carrying out instructions

Dear Sir

[*insert appropriate heading*]

Thank you for your letter of [*insert date*].

I have carefully considered your proposals to complete the work detailed in my instruction number [*insert number*] dated [*insert date*]. I cannot agree to your proposals.

The notice sent to you on [*insert date*] will shortly expire and you are strongly urged to put the work in hand before that date to avoid the employer taking action to employ others to do the work at considerable extra cost to yourself.

[*If the notice has already expired by the time you write this letter, omit the last paragraph and substitute the three paragraphs of letter* **64**.]

Yours faithfully

Copies: Employer
　　　　　Quantity surveyor

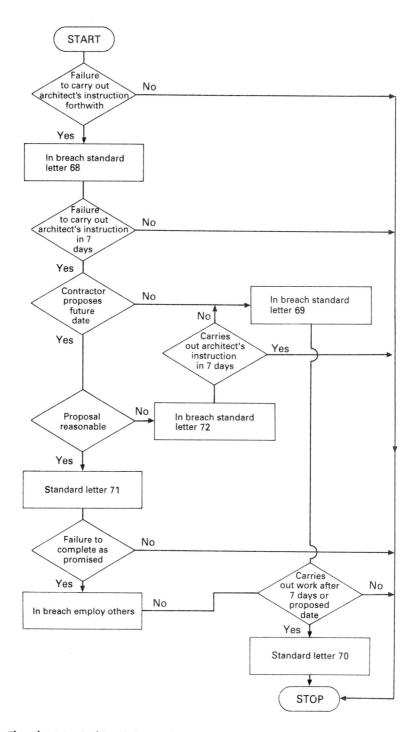

Flowchart 1 Architect's instructions.

pliance notice in similar terms to that of the standard form but no provision for the contractor to object (except of course by arbitration). Letters **68** to **72** inclusive are applicable as are the other general remarks in this section. **Flowchart 1** is also appropriate.

If the contractor continues to default, you should record the fact **(69)**.

Employer: accepts new quotation

You can proceed to arrange for the work to be done by the others. If you decide to take this action, and there may not be any alternative, it is advisable to obtain three quotations for carrying out the work if the work in question lends itself to this method of approach. The reason is because, in recovering costs from the contractor, you ought to be able to show that the employer has made reasonable efforts to have the work done at the lowest practicable price. In the case of an instruction for additional work, you will be seeking to recover costs which will be the difference between the actual cost and the contractor's bill rates, plus incidental costs which can include your additional fees. You will have to use your discretion as to whether the time scale of the work allows you to seek quotations.

Complications occur if the contractor carries out the instruction at the thirteenth hour, after the employer has already accepted a quotation from another firm **(70)**.

Note that all communications to the contractor must spell out precisely four points:

- ❑ Relevant dates
- ❑ Relevant clauses of the conditions
- ❑ Failure by contractor
- ❑ Financial consequences to the contractor

Contractor: seeks to agree new date

After receipt of your notice to comply in accordance with clause 4.1.2, it is not unusual for the contractor to claim that he has not carried out your instruction forthwith because it does not fit in with his work programme. He may, however, promise to carry out the work by a specific date. You must consider all aspects of the contract carefully before agreeing to his proposal, being careful to preserve the employer's rights **(72)**. In most cases you will probably reject his suggestions.

It is never easy to decide to employ others on the contractor's work. It sours relationships. Generally, it is less damaging when the project is almost complete rather than in the initial stages.

K14 Instructions: by building control officer (73), (74, (75), (Flowchart 2)

The building control officer will inspect the works in progress as part of his natural duties. Although not empowered to do so, if he finds anything which is not in accordance with the building regulations, he will very often give oral instructions to the person-in-charge on site to correct the problem. The contractor may carry out the instruction and present the result to you as a *fait accompli*, demanding extra payment. You should adopt a procedure best illustrated by **Flowchart 2**. (The clause numbers on the flowchart are only applicable to the standard form.)

IFC 84

Statutory obligations are covered by clauses 5.1–5.3. Emergency compliance is covered by clause 5.4. **Flowchart 2** and letters **73** to **75** are applicable.

MW 80

Clause 5.1 deals with statutory obligations. There is no procedure for emergencies. The contractor, however, may claim an emergency. Letters **73** to **75** inclusive are applicable with the amendments indicated. **Flowchart 2** relates to the standard form but it may be used as a general guide to the procedure you can adopt to decide whether there was an emergency and to what extent the contractor must bear the costs.

A similar procedure would be suitable if any other statutory authority was concerned.

K15 Setting out: architect requested to check (76), (77), (78), (79), (instruction 1)

Clause 7 requires you to determine any levels required for the execution of the works and to supply accurately dimensioned drawings so that the contractor can set out the works at ground level.

It is common for the contractor to request the architect to check his setting out. The architect normally complies and will often confirm the accuracy. It is an extremely dangerous thing to do because it tends to relieve the contractor of his responsibility for errors. It is, of course, quite sensible for you to carry out any dimensional checks on site if you

73 Letter from architect to contractor if contractor complies with building control officer's instruction to correct his own error

Dear Sir

[*insert appropriate heading*]

Thank you for your letter of [*insert date*].

I cannot consider your claim for additional costs in complying with the instructions of the building control officer because the defect you corrected is one which would not have occurred if you had carried out the work in accordance with the contract.

Yours faithfully

Copy: Quantity surveyor

74 Letter from architect to contractor if contractor complies with building control officer's instruction to correct error due to divergence between statutory requirements and contract documents, not constituting an emergency

Dear Sir

[*insert appropriate heading*]

I cannot consider your claim for additional costs, submitted on [*insert date*], in complying with the instructions of the building control officers for the following reasons:

1   Although the defect was allegedly due to a divergence between the contract documents and statutory requirements,
   (a)   the situation did not fall into the category of an emergency envisaged by clause 6.1.4.1[1]
   (b)   it fell under clause 6.1.2[2] and you failed to give me the required written notice specifying the divergence; therefore
2   I had no opportunity to issue appropriate instructions, and
3   Your action was your responsibility and your cost.

Yours faithfully

Copy: Quantity surveyor

---

[1]   *Substitute '5.4' when using IFC 84. Omit when using MW 80*
[2]   *Substitute '5.2' when using IFC 84. Omit when using MW 80*

75 Letter from architect to contractor if he has not complied with all the provisions of clause 6.1.4.1 and 2 (or 5.4.1 and 5.4.2 when using IFC 84)

Dear Sir

[*insert appropriate heading*]

Thank you for your letter of [*insert date*].

In carrying out the work instructed by the building control officer I accept that the situation was an emergency envisaged by clause 6.1.4.1.[1]

However, you did not [*omit one of the following phrases as appropriate*] supply limited materials and execute limited work in accordance with clause 6.1.4.1[1]/forthwith inform me of the emergency and the steps you were taking as required by clause 6.1.4.2.[2]

In the circumstances, the claim you are making for additional cost will be allowed subject to a deduction for unnecessary expense due to your default(s).

Yours faithfully

Copy: Quantity surveyor

---

[1] *Substitute '5.4.1' when using IFC 84*
Omit underlined phrase when using MW 80
[2] *Substitute '5.4.2' when using IFC 84*
Omit underlined phrase when using MW 80

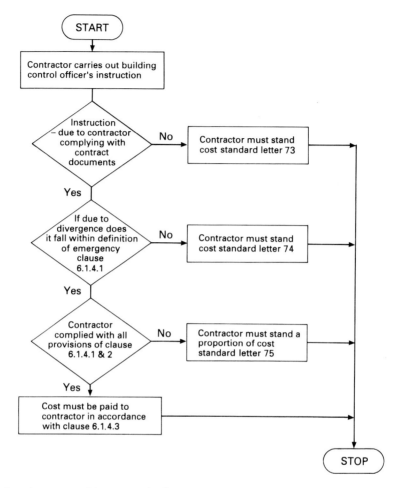

Flowchart 2 Building control officer's instructions.

wish in order to fulfil your obligations to your client. Be quite clear, however, that you are carrying out your own duties and not those of the contractor **(76)**.

If you do visit the site and check the setting out for your own peace of mind, it is not unusual for you to receive a letter from the contractor recording your visit and confirming that you have found their setting out to be correct **(77)**.

The contractor is responsible for correcting errors in his own setting out at no cost to the employer. It may be convenient, perhaps because the error is not great or because time is short, to instruct the contractor not to amend erroneous setting out. You must obtain the employer's consent first. An appropriate deduction may be made from the contract sum. The precise method of arriving at the figure is not set out in

76 Letter from architect to contractor replying to request to check setting out

Dear Sir

[*insert appropriate heading*]

Thank you for your letter of [*insert date*].

The setting out of the works on site is your responsibility under the contract. I am of the opinion that you have been provided with all necessary dimensions and such information as to enable you to do so. Any inspection I may decide to carry out will not remove your obligations, neither will any lack of comment on my part imply approval of your setting out.

Yours faithfully

77 Letter from architect to contractor replying to confirmation that setting out is correct

Dear Sir

[*insert appropriate heading*]

Thank you for your letter of [*insert date*].

The setting out of the works on site is your responsibility <u>in accordance with clause 7 of the conditions of contract</u>.[1] Any inspection which I make, including the taking of dimensions as I deem appropriate, does not relieve you of your responsibilities in any way.

I have not confirmed and do not confirm that your setting out is correct. Any lack of comment from me is not to be taken, in this or any other matter, to be a sign of approval.

Yours faithfully

---

[1]   *Substitute '3.9' when using IFC 84*
      Omit underlined phrase when using MW 80

78 Letter from architect to contractor informing him of the amount to be deducted for errors in setting out

Not suitable for use with MW 80

Dear Sir

[*insert appropriate heading*]

I refer to my instruction number [*insert number*] dated [*insert date*] regarding an error in setting out.

The amount to be deducted from the contract sum in respect of the inaccurate setting out is £[*insert amount*]. This sum represents an appropriate deduction.

Yours faithfully

79 Letter from architect to contractor if contractor wishes to correct inaccurate setting out

Not suitable for use with MW 80

Dear Sir

[*insert appropriate heading*]

Thank you for your letter of [*insert date*].

[*Then, either:*]

I note that you wish to amend the inaccurate setting out noted in my instruction number [*insert number*] dated [*insert date*]. I am please to consent to your request provided that [*insert any conditions you wish to impose, such as date by which the amendment must be complete, safety of adjacent work, etc.*]. Such amendment must be carried out entirely at your own cost with no damage to any other part of the works and on the basis that you will have no claim for any loss and/or expense or extension of time in respect of such amendment. This consent and your corrective works are not to be construed as relieving you from any of your obligations under the contract.

[*Or:*]

The instruction to which you refer was issued after having carefully considered the consequences of amending the error at this stage of the work. The employer has decided to exercise his right to consent to my instruction that the error not be amended. Your duty is to comply with my instruction forthwith. I know you are concerned regarding the amount to be deducted from the contract sum and I should be happy to discuss this aspect with you. Perhaps you would care to telephone me later in the week to arrange a meeting?

Yours faithfully

Architect's instruction 1: not to amend error in setting out

Not suitable for use with MW 80

Refer to the attached drawing number [*insert number*]. An error in setting out is apparent in the position marked A. The approximate line of the inaccurate setting out of this portion of the work is indicated on the drawing by the red line superimposed over the printed information. With the consent of the employer in accordance with clause 7[1] I instruct you not to amend such inaccurate setting out. An appropriate deduction will be made from the contract sum.

---

[1]   *Substitute '3.9' when using IFC 84*

the contract. It cannot be the cost of getting others to correct the setting out. In certain circumstances, it may be what it would have cost the contractor to correct the setting out. If the employer is very little or not at all inconvenienced by the error, an appropriate deduction may be nothing at all or a relatively nominal sum. This provision does give the employer the opportunity to make an unexpected profit. The quantity surveyor is to do the calculation (clause 30.2.3.1) and it is reasonable for you to inform the contractor of the amount to be deducted as soon as possible **(78)**. What if the contractor replies, saying the deduction is outrageous and he will correct the setting out instead? **(79)**.

IFC 84

Setting out is covered by clause 3.9.

MW 80

There is no specific mention of setting out, but it is a necessary implication that you will supply all the information and the contractor has responsibility, as part of his work, for setting out. The general remarks in this section are applicable as are letters **76** and **77** with amendments as indicated.

K16 Defective work: dealing with the problem (80), (81), (instruction 2)

The contractor's obligations are set down very concisely in clause 2.1. Problems sometimes arise if the work, materials or goods are defective. To be defective they must be 'not in accordance with (the) contract'.

Defects are normally discovered by the contractor, the clerk of works or the architect. Most defects are corrected before anyone but the contractor notices. Defects found by the clerk of works and architect are normally mentioned and recorded in a clerk of works site direction. Usually that is sufficient but, if the defect is serious or the contractor shows any reluctance to attend to it immediately, it is wise to issue an instruction to cover the matter.

The normal instruction is to remove the defective goods, materials or work from site. You are not empowered by the conditions simply to require a defect occurring during the course of the work to be made good. You do have other options. If the employer agrees, you can allow the defect to remain and an appropriate deduction must be made

80 Letter from architect to contractor if contractor objects to instruction to open up or test after non-compliance discovered

This letter is not suitable for use with IFC 84 or MW 80

Dear Sir

[*insert appropriate heading*]

Thank you for your letter of [*insert date*] and I note that you object to carrying out the opening up/testing [*delete as appropriate*] described in my instruction number [*insert number*] dated [*insert date*] issued pursuant to clause 8.4.4 of the conditions of contract.

The instruction was issued after I had had due regard to the code of practice appended to the conditions and you should comply with the instruction forthwith.

Yours faithfully

81 Letter from architect to contractor after discovery of work not in accordance with the contract

This letter is not suitable for use with JCT 80 or MW 80

Dear Sir

[*insert appropriate heading*]

When visiting site today, I noted that [*describe the work or materials*] failed to be in accordance with the contract.

In accordance with clause 3.13.1 of the conditions of contract, I require you to state in writing within seven days of the date of this letter the action you will immediately take at no cost to the employer to establish that there is no similar failure in work already executed/materials or goods already supplied [*delete as appropriate*].

Yours faithfully

Architect's instruction 2: to remove defective works, materials or goods

The following work/materials/goods [*omit as appropriate*] are not in accordance with the contract and must be removed from site <u>in accordance with clause 8.4.</u>[1]

[*List defects*]

Copies: Quantity surveyor
Clerk of works

---

[1] *Substitute '3.14' when using IFC 84*
Omit underlined phrase when using MW 80

when the contract sum is adjusted. The sum in this instance is usually what it would cost the contractor to make good. You must consult with the contractor first and confirm the position in writing.

Removal of defective work sometimes means that it is desirable to issue a further instruction to vary other work. Insofar as the further instruction is reasonably necessary as a result of ordering removal of work (or of allowing defective work to remain), clause 8.4.3 permits issue without any resultant addition to the contract sum or extension of the contract period. You must consult with the contractor first. If he objects to the amount or kind of variation you propose to order, there is no contractual mechanism to give any weight to his objection except that he may seek arbitration. The arbitration will not be opened until after practical completion unless he can bring the reference within the question of whether an instruction is empowered by the conditions. Probably, there is little doubt about that. The crucial question for the contractor is one of money and time.

Clause 8.4.4 allows you to go further and issue instructions to open up and test part of the works to establish to your reasonable satisfaction that there are no similar defects or, as appropriate, that the defect is no greater in extent than you have already discovered. Provided that the opening up required is reasonable, there is to be no addition to the contract sum whatever the result. The contractor may be entitled to an extension of time under clause 25.4.5.2 if the opening up showed that the materials, goods or workmanship was in accordance with the contract. What is reasonable will depend on circumstances. In order to help you to decide, a code of practice is appended to the conditions to which you must 'have due regard' before issuing your instruction. Clearly, if you can agree with the contractor the opening up required to demonstrate that the remainder of the works contains no similar defect, that is ideal. The contractor should be anxious to satisfy you on that point. If you cannot agree, you may proceed whether the contractor agrees or not. In any subsequent arbitration, the degree to which you took into account the matters in the code of practice would determine to what extent your instruction was reasonable 'in all the circumstances'. If the contractor objects, you should make the position clear to him (80).

If the contractor does not carry out the instruction, you should follow the normal procedure outlined in K13.

IFC 84

You may instruct removal of work by virtue of clause 3.14. After that, the system is different from JCT 80. When work or material are discovered to be not in accordance with the contract, the onus is on the contractor to give a written statement to you telling you what he proposes to do at no cost to the employer to establish that similar work is not similarly affected. You may issue your own instructions to him to open up or test the work if:

❑ The contractor has not sent you his proposals within seven days of the discovery of the defect; *or*
❑ You are not satisfied with them; *or*
❑ For safety or statutory reasons you cannot wait for his proposals.

The contractor has ten days after he receives your instruction to give you written objection with reasons. If you do not withdraw your instruction or modify it to remove his objection within seven days of receipt of his objection, the matter is referred to immediate arbitration. The contractor is not excused from complying with the instruction and the usual sanctions (see **K13**) are applicable. The extent to which the arbitrator finds that your instruction is not fair and reasonable will determine the amount of payment by the employer and the contractor's entitlement to an extension of time.

   One of the problems with this clause is that the obligation laid on the contractor does not distinguish the severity of the defect. Thus, in theory, the contractor should give you his proposals for every defect discovered no matter how small. You have no power to waive this requirement, neither would it be wise to do so, but it makes sense to achieve a clear understanding with the contractor about what it means in practice. An appropriate forum for doing this is the pre-start meeting. It is quite likely that the contractor will consider that only really major defects warrant the application of this clause so you should prompt him whenever you become aware of a defect **(81)**.

MW 80

There is no specific provision for dealing with defective work as the contract progresses but it must be implied that you can issue instructions to deal with any work not in accordance with the contract by virtue of clause 3.5. There are no provisions for ordering, opening up or testing after failure of work, but of course there is no reason why you should not so instruct provided you are willing to take the risk that the work will be in accordance with the contract and an addition must be made to the contract sum. Architect's instruction 2 is applicable.

K17 Defective work: late instructions to remove (82), (83), (84), (85)

More often than you may care to admit, defects are discovered on site long after subsequent work has been completed (e.g. windows built in too low or too high). In such cases you will, no doubt, do everything you can to see whether the work can be made acceptable without too much additional cost to the contractor. You will try particularly hard if it comes into the category known as 'honest mistakes'. If you decide that something, other than the work or materials required by the contract, is acceptable you must obtain the employer's consent and make sure that the contractor is in the position of offering a solution at his own risk and taking full design responsibility for it, if appropriate. The trouble is that, although you may know what you would like to see done, you must beware of giving the contractor anything which can be construed as an instruction. For this purpose the device of the double letter is helpful **(82), (83)**.

The two letters are sent to the contractor at the same time.

After receiving the instruction to remove defective work, the contractor may put forward various objections. He may allege, among other things:

❏ The defective work, while admittedly not quite what was required, has been in position for a considerable time and it is unreasonable to order its removal so late in the contract
❏ The architect and clerk of works did not make any adverse comment during many inspections
❏ The contractor was led to assume approval by the conduct of the architect and clerk of works
❏ The architect and the clerk of works deliberately waited until the last moment to condemn defective work because the employer will not be ready to occupy the works at the contractual completion date

It is important to remember that the contractor is probably quite sincere in his accusations. From his point of view it is catastrophic to be told, for example, that the floor-to-ceiling heights are incorrect when the shell of the building is complete. Nevertheless, the position should be made quite clear to him **(84)**. The question really is whether the contractor has done what he undertook to do in the contract. If not, he is in breach. Having said that, there are circumstances where the cost of remedying a breach will far outweigh any possible advantage and the law will then look at what is reasonable in all the circumstances.

82 Letter from architect to contractor (double letter 1)

Dear Sir

[*insert appropriate heading*]

I refer to my instruction number [*insert number*] dated [*insert date*] requiring removal of defective work and to your letter of [*insert date*] asking if there is some other way of dealing with the defect.

I am always ready to consider your suggestions, but it is for you to put forward your proposals and confirm that you are prepared to accept full responsibility for the results. They must be at no further cost to the contract and you must accept that the employer reserves the right to change back to the original specification.

Yours faithfully

83 Letter from architect to contractor (double letter 2)

WITHOUT PREJUDICE

Dear Sir

[*insert appropriate heading*]

With regard to the defect specified in my instruction number [*insert number*] dated [*insert date*], if you were to suggest the following, I should be prepared to accept it:

[*State precisely what you wish the contractor to submit to you as his suggestion.*]

Yours faithfully

84 Letter from architect to contractor countering allegation that late instruction implies approval

Dear Sir

[*insert appropriate heading*]

In reply to your letter of [*insert date*], the position with regard to defective work or materials is quite clear. It is your responsibility under the contract to ensure that the works are properly executed. The duty of the clerk of works is to inspect on behalf of the employer. He is not on site to carry out any of the duties of your own person-in-charge.

Neither I nor the clerk of works has any duty to inform you of defects at any particular time. Lack of comment can never be taken to indicate approval.

[*The next paragraph may be added at your discretion:*]

I recognise that you will suffer a heavy financial burden in carrying out my instruction number [*insert number*]. Without prejudice to the position already stated and the effect of the above-mentioned instructions, I am prepared to consider any alternative proposals you submit within the next week.

Yours faithfully

Note: References to the clerk of works should be omitted when using MW 80 if no clerk of works is employed

85   Letter from architect to contractor if contractor quotes clause 8.2.2

This letter is not suitable for use with IFC 84 or MW 80

Dear Sir

[*insert appropriate heading*]

Thank you for your letter of [*insert date*] in which, on the basis of clause 8.2.2, you object to my instruction number [*insert number*] dated [*insert date*] requiring you to remove [*list defects*] from site under the provisions of clause 8.4.1.

In the case of work falling under the second part of clause 2.1, clause 8.2.2 requires me to express any dissatisfaction within a reasonable time from the execution of the unsatisfactory work. What is a reasonable time cannot be considered in the abstract, but must be viewed in the light of all the circumstances. It is my opinion that I have expressed my dissatisfaction within a reasonable time in this instance. Please carry out the above noted instruction number [*insert number*] forthwith.

Yours faithfully

Suppose the contractor quotes clause 8.2.2 in his favour because the defect is in work which is specified to be to your 'approval' or 'satisfaction'. Your reply will depend upon precise circumstances, but letter **85** may be appropriate.

IFC 84 and MW 80

The comments are generally applicable to these forms except that there is no equivalent to clause 8.2.2.

K18 Materials, goods and workmanship: not procurable (86), (87), (88), (89)

At some stage in almost every contract, the contractor will write informing you that some materials are not procurable. He will usually suggest something else. His letter may mean:

❑ Materials not procurable at the price he originally envisaged
❑ Materials not procurable at the appropriate time (possibly because he was late in placing his order)
❑ Materials not procurable because they have gone out of production since he submitted his tender

The position is as follows:

❑ The contractor must pay the higher price and stand the difference if that is the problem
❑ If he was late in placing his order, he must stand the difference in cost of any reasonable alternative you allow him to use
❑ If the delivery date is just impossibly long or the materials have gone out of production, you must specify an alternative and the contract sum must be adjusted accordingly

Before you arrive at any decision you must be certain of your facts. It is wise to write to both contractor and supplier. If you are lucky, your letters will result in the materials becoming available as if by magic. The alternative result will be that you will have sufficient information to make the decision on the merits of the case.

IFC 84 and MW 80

The contractor's obligations are not similarly qualified under these forms. The result is probably that if materials are not procurable, the

86 Letter from architect to contractor if materials not procurable

Dear Sir

[*insert appropriate heading*]

Thank you for your letter of [*insert date*].

Before I can make a decision on this matter, I should be pleased if you would supply me with the following information:

1   The date on which you placed your order.

2   Photostat copies of your order and any correspondence between the supplier and yourself.

3   Details of your attempts to obtain the materials from an alternative supplier.

Yours faithfully

87   Letter from architect to supplier if materials not procurable

Dear Sir

[*insert appropriate heading*]

I am informed by [*insert name of main contractor*] that you are unable to supply [*insert name or description of material*] which is specified in this contract and is required on site on [*insert date*]. I should be grateful if you would confirm the position and let me have the following information:

1   The date on which you received the contractor's order.

2   Any other information which might be relevant, e.g. delivery period.

Needless to say, I view the situation with concern, and your reply will obviously affect not only this contract but my specifying policy in the future.

Yours faithfully

88   Letter from architect to contractor if he is to stand the extra costs of alternative materials

Dear Sir

[*insert appropriate heading*]

I have now had the opportunity to consider your letters of [*insert dates of all the contractor's letters bearing on the subject*]. I have also made my own enquiries.

I am prepared to agree to your suggestion that the following alternative materials be used at no additional cost to the contract arising either directly or indirectly from their use.

[*List the materials you are prepared to accept.*]

My agreement is on the clear understanding that you will accept full responsibility for the suitability and performance of the said materials.

Yours faithfully

89 Letter from architect to contractor if he is to be allowed any additional costs for alternative materials

Dear Sir

[*insert appropriate heading*]

I have considered your letters of [*insert dates of all the contractor's letters bearing on the subject*]. I have also made my own enquiries.

I am prepared to agree to the use of the following alternative materials.

[*List any materials you are prepared to accept.*]

Additional costs, if any, will be agreed between the respective quantity surveyors.[1]

Yours faithfully

Copy: Quantity surveyor

---

[1] *Substitute 'decided by me in due course' when using MW 80*

contractors must obtain your consent to the provision of substitute materials at no additional cost to the employer. Letter **88** is applicable.

K19 Inspection of work covered up (90), (instruction 3)

The contract (clause 8.3) is clear that you may order the opening up of any work for inspection, but the cost of opening up and making good again will be added to the contract sum unless the work is not in accordance with the contract.

It is vital that you arrange for any such inspection to take place on a certain day and time and arrange to be present (with the clerk of works if there is one) to watch the opening up of the work.

IFC 84

Opening up and inspection or testing is covered by clause 3.12 in similar terms.

MW 80

Clause 3.5 allows you to issue any written instructions. The remarks, architect's instruction 3 and letter **90** in this section can be regarded as a general indication of reasonable practice. The instruction should protect you against the contractor opening up and correcting the work before you arrive.

If the work is, in fact, defective, you must immediately confirm the fact **(90)**, otherwise the contractor may confirm the contrary and an argument will develop in which he who fires the first shot may be victorious.

K20 Person-in-charge: non-notification (91)

A competent person-in-charge must be constantly present on the site. The name of this person (in a contract of any size it will be the site agent or foreman) will have been notified to you at the commencement of the contract.

The contractor may change the person-in-charge without notifying you. It does happen from time to time for various reasons. You must take a very firm stand because it is essential that you know:

90 Letter from architect to contractor confirming the opening up of defective work

Dear Sir

[*insert appropriate heading*]

Together with [*name of contractor's representative*], I attended the opening up of [*specify exactly the portion of the works opened up*] at [*insert time*] on [*insert date*]. (The clerk of works was also present [*if applicable*].)

The work was found to be not in accordance with the contract. An instruction is enclosed under clause 8.4[1] requiring removal.

When you consider the work to have been executed in accordance with the contract, the clerk of works[2] must be allowed to inspect before making good takes place.

In accordance with clause 8.3[3], the cost of opening up and making good is to be at your expense.

Yours faithfully

Copies: Quantity surveyor
Clerk of works [*if applicable*]

---

[1] *Substitute '3.14' when using IFC 84*
Omit when using MW 80
[2] *Substitute 'I' when using MW 80*
[3] *Substitute '3.12' when using IFC 84*
Omit when using MW 80

Architect's instruction 3: requiring work to be opened up

In accordance with clause 8.3[1] of the conditions of contract, I require you to open up [*specify the exact portion of the works you require to be opened up*] for inspection (and testing [*if applicable*]). I intend to be present (with the clerk of works [*if applicable*]) to observe.

The work must be carried out at [*insert time*] on [*insert date*]. No opening up must begin before the time stipulated.

Failure to comply strictly with this instruction will result in you having to bear the cost of opening up and making good whatever the outcome of the inspection.

Copies: Quantity surveyor
Clerk of works [*if applicable*]

---

[1] *Substitute '3.12' when using IFC 84*
Substitute '3.5' when using MW 80

91 Letter from architect to contractor requesting the name of person-in-charge

Dear Sir

[*insert appropriate heading*]

Clause 10 of the conditions of contract requires you to keep constantly upon the works a competent person-in charge.[1] On [*insert date*] you notified me that this person would be [*insert name*].

It has come to my attention that [*insert name*] is no longer on site.[2] If you have no person-in-charge, you are in breach of contract. I will assume that is not the case. Please notify me of the appointment and identity of the person-in-charge. Until you inform me of his identity, I am unable to issue instructions on site with any certainty. Any consideration of your entitlement to extension of time or loss and/or expense on this contract will take such matters into account.

Yours faithfully

Copies: Quantity surveyor
Clerk of works [*if applicable*]

---

[1] *With IFC 84 the first paragraph should read: 'Clause 3.4 of the conditions of contract requires you at all reasonable times to keep upon the works a competent person-in-charge'*
With MW 80 the first paragraph should read: 'Clause 3.3 of the conditions of contract requires you at all reasonable times to keep upon the works a competent person-in-charge'
[2] *With IFC 84 and MW 80 add: 'at all reasonable times'*

❑ That there is a person-in-charge
❑ His identity, so that he can be given instructions

IFC 84 and MW 80

The contractor must keep a competent person-in-charge upon the works at all reasonable times. It would be unreasonable to expect a foreman to be on site constantly on a very small job. However, it is reasonable for you to know the name of the person-in-charge and the general remarks and letter **91** in this section are applicable.

K21 Variations: change in scope and character of the work (92)

One of the important reasons for the 'variation clause' is to prevent the contract being put at an end by an instruction to the contractor to alter or modify the works in some way. Clause 13.2 specifically mentions the point. If it were not for this clause, a relatively minor alteration would necessitate a renegotiation of the contract.

Sometimes, if a contractor is falling behind in his programme and/or losing money, he will try to argue that the contract is at an end and should be renegotiated because the variations have altered the whole scope and character of the work. If the variations have had this effect, the contractor would be right in his assertion despite clause 13.3. All rests upon what the parties contemplated and expressed as their intentions in the contract.

For example, if the contract was to build one house and you issued a variation to add another similar house, it would vitiate the original contract because you have increased the scope of the work by 100% and the contract would be different from that which the contractor undertook to carry out. If, however, the contract was to build one hundred houses and you issued a variation to add one house, it would be unlikely to vitiate the contract because you have increased the scope by a mere 1% and it is the same contract with a minor variation to the work. To get at the principle you must consider that the first contract was doubled in scope but the second contract was increased fractionally.

An extreme case of altering the character of the work would be to issue a variation altering a factory into a school. Such a measure would clearly vitiate the contract.

You are unlikely to have taken such drastic steps as regards scope or character but you are almost certain to have issued a number of

92   Letter from architect to contractor if he alleges scope and character of the work changed

Dear Sir

[*insert appropriate heading*]

I received your communication of the [*insert date*] and I totally reject any suggestion that the whole scope and character of the work has been changed.[1]

If you persist in this attempt to repudiate the contract, the consequences will be very serious for you.

Yours faithfully

Copy: Quantity surveyor

---

[1]   *Use the contractor's own words*

instructions requiring minor variations. The contractor usually bases his case on the fact that clause 13.2 refers to variation in the singular. In others words 'no variation' shall vitiate the contract, but variations might. He will argue that the total variations you have issued have, taken together, changed the scope and character of the work. He would be correct if your variations had, little by little, altered virtually every detail of your building.

Fortunately, such situations are rare. He would be unlikely to succeed in any action he might bring. You must be firm.

IFC 84

Clause 3.6 also provides that no instruction or sanction of a variation will vitiate the contract and the comments also apply to this form.

MW 80

Clause 3.6 refers to the architect ordering an addition to or an omission from or other change in the works without 'invalidating' the contract. This is basically the same as vitiating the contract as noted in the standard form. The contractor may still base his case on the singular, i.e. 'an addition' etc. The general remarks are applicable as is letter **92**.

K22 Practical completion: alleged by contractor (93)

In order to secure the release of half the retention money and relieve him of the continuous presence of men and plant on site, the contractor will sometimes write alleging that the works are suitable for occupation, although not every detail is complete and, therefore, practical completion should be certified.

The certification is entirely a matter for your discretion, but your discretion must be exercised within certain parameters. Practical completion does not mean 'almost complete'. The consensus of judicial view appears to be that the certificate may be issued if there are still some very minor works incomplete, but not if there are any obvious defects. A useful way of defining it can be that the works have reached a high degree of completion such that the employer can occupy the premises fully, without suffering any inconvenience from workmen putting the finishing touches to the works. Such a situation might arise, for example, if some of the external works only remain to be completed.

93 Letter from architect to contractor regarding practical completion

Dear Sir

[*insert appropriate heading*]

Thank you for your letter of [*insert date*].

I inspected the works today and in my opinion practical completion has not yet been achieved. Items are still outstanding. Among other things are:

[*List some of the things you noticed.*]

The above is not a comprehensive list. It is for you to ensure that the works are completed in accordance with the contract. I expect you to have carried out a thorough check before you inform me that the works are ready for practical completion to be certified.

Yours faithfully

Copy: Quantity surveyor

If you decide that practical completion has not been reached, you must tell the contractor. There is no reason why you should not note one or two items still outstanding, but beware of preparing long lists of defects at this stage. The contractor knows what is to be done and it is for him to carry out his own checks to ensure that the work is finished and all defects are corrected.

K23 Postponement: claimed implied in instructions (94), (95)

You are entitled to issue instructions to postpone the work under clause 23.3 of the conditions. The contractor is entitled to loss and/or expense due to such postponement (clause 26.2.5). Therefore, you will be reluctant to issue postponement instructions. What is the position if the contractor claims that your instructions on some other matter effectively imply postponement?

Although it is possible that instructions to deal with defective work or nominate sub-contractors, etc. may constitute postponement instructions, it is more likely that what he is really saying is that your instructions have caused delay, which is quite another matter and may only entitle him to an extension of time.

Case law suggests that the courts will treat each situation on its merits. Try not to anticipate an adverse judgment. Your best move is to state your position clearly for the benefit of the contractor and the record.

IFC 84

Postponement is governed by clause 3.15 and any loss and/or expense would be reimbursed under clause 4.12.5.

MW 80

There are no specific provisions for postponement. The general remarks in this section are applicable but a different letter is required. Letter **95** should be used.

94 Letter from architect to contractor regarding alleged postponement

This letter is not suitable for use with MW 80

Dear Sir

[*insert appropriate heading*]

Thank you for your letter of [*insert date*].

There are specific provisions for postponement in clause 23.2 of the conditions.

I have issued no postponement instructions in accordance with clause 23.2 or otherwise and I do not intend to do so in connection with the matter to which you refer.

If you wish to make any claims under this contract, you must submit them in accordance with the provisions of the contract when they will receive proper consideration.

Yours faithfully

Copy: Quantity surveyor

95   Letter from architect to contractor regarding alleged postponement

This letter is suitable only for use with MW 80

Dear Sir

[*insert appropriate heading*]

Thank you for your letter of [*insert date*].

I have issued instructions in accordance with clause 3.5/3.6/3.7 [*omit as appropriate*]. My instructions do not imply, nor are they intended to imply, postponement.

There is no specific provision for postponement in this contract.

Yours faithfully

K24 Liquidated damages: objections by contractor (96)

If you certify that the contractor has failed to complete the works by the completion date, the employer is entitled to deduct liquidated and ascertained damages in accordance with clause 24.

The contractor will sometimes raise the objection that the sum stated in the appendix is not a true reflection of the damage suffered by the employer and it is, therefore, a penalty and cannot be enforced.

There is a great deal of misapprehension about this particular aspect of the contract. Broadly, penalties cannot be enforced; liquidated and ascertained damages can. Because it is notoriously difficult to ascertain damages after the event, and expensive to apply them, the contract adopts the device of agreed damages. Provided that you have considered the amount of damages with the employer, made a genuine pre-estimate of the loss the employer could suffer and included the amount in the bills of quantities (or specification) sent to the contractor at tender stage, those damages can be applied. It matters not whether the actual loss is greater or less. The important point is that the liquidated and ascertained damages were a reasonable estimate at the time the contract was made.

A penalty is something imposed as a punishment out of all proportion to the loss expected, or one sum payable on the occurrence of any one of dissimilar events. For example, if you were dealing with a private house, reasonable damages might be composed of the weekly cost of renting something similar plus additional removal expenses and incidental costs. It might even be the cost of an hotel room, and you should always include something for your additional fees.

Once calculated and put in the contract, liquidated and ascertained damages do not have to be justified to the contractor before they can be applied. Obviously, you must be prepared to justify them to an arbitrator if the contractor should take things to that point. Even then, you have only to justify your method of calculation, not whether the damages are accurate at the end of the job.

It sometimes happens that you go out to tender without inserting any sum as liquidated damages. If this occurs, you are not simply entitled to insert a suitable sum in the form of contract before it is signed. The position is that the contractor has agreed to carry out the work on terms, one of which is that the amount of liquidated damages is nothing. In order to be able to put something in the contract, it must first be agreed with the contractor. Doubtless he would require an increase in his tender figure for his agreement. If the employer wishes to be able to sue for such damages as he has actually suffered, the

96 Letter from architect to contractor regarding liquidated damages

Dear Sir

[*insert appropriate heading*]

I have received your letter of [*insert date*] and read the contents with surprise.

Liquidated and ascertained damages are intended to be a genuine pre-estimate of damage to avoid just the sort of dispute you are endeavouring to start.

Neither the employer nor I intend to enter into any discussion with you on the subject. I will only confirm that the sum entered in the contract was a genuine pre-estimate of damage.

Yours faithfully

Copies: Employer
        Quantity surveyor

liquidated damages clause in the contract must be entirely struck out and initialled by both parties.

IFC 84

Liquidated damages are referred to in clause 2.7. In other respects this section is applicable.

MW 80

Liquidated damages are referred to in clause 2.3. In other respects this section is applicable.

K25 Determination: by employer (97), (98), (99), (100) (flowcharts 3, 4, 5)

Determination of the contractor's employment under the contract is something best avoided if possible. If you decide, with the employer, that it is to be done, it must be done in the proper way, and the process is fraught with difficulties. However, the party properly determining the contractor's employment is legally and financially in the best position provided it is done for a sufficient reason. Flowchart 3 indicates the procedure.

Clauses 27, 28A and 22C.4.3 govern determination by the employer. They can be considered in two parts, the *grounds* for determination and the *procedure after* determination.

Grounds for determination

The grounds in clause 27 are divided into a group of four and two separate grounds. The first four are the contractor:

❏ Wholly suspending the works without reasonable cause
❏ Failing to proceed regularly and diligently
❏ Refusing or neglecting to comply with a written notice requiring him to remove defective work or improper materials or goods and thereby the works being materially affected
❏ Failing to comply with clause 19 (assignments and sub-contracts)

If it is decided to determine on any of the above four grounds, you must first give the contractor a notice by registered post or recorded delivery specifying the default **(97)**. If the default is continued for 14 days after receipt of the notice, you may draw up a letter for the

97   Letter from architect to contractor giving notice of default

This letter is not suitable for use with MW 80

REGISTERED POST/RECORDED DELIVERY [*as appropriate*]

Dear Sir

[*insert appropriate heading*]

I hereby give you notice under clause 27.2[1] of the conditions of contract that you are in default in the following respect:

[*Insert details of the default with dates if appropriate.*]

If you continue the default for 14 days after receipt of this notice or if you at any time repeat such default (whether previously repeated or not) the employer may <u>within 10 days of such continuance or repetition</u>[2] forthwith determine your employment under this contract without further notice.

Yours faithfully

Copies: Employer
            Quantity surveyor

---

[1]   *Substitute '7.1' when using IFC 84*
[2]   *Omit the portion underlined when using IFC 84*

98 Letter from employer to contractor determining employment

This letter is not suitable for use with MW 80

REGISTERED POST/RECORDED DELIVERY [*as appropriate*]

Dear Sir

[*insert appropriate heading*]

I refer to the notice dated [*insert date of original notice*] sent to you by the architect.

In accordance with clause 27.2.2[1] of the conditions of contract take this as notice that I hereby forthwith determine your employment under this contract without prejudice to any other rights or remedies which I may possess.

The rights and duties of the parties are governed by clauses 27.6 and 27.7.[2] No temporary building, plant, tools, equipment, goods or materials may be removed from the site until (and if) the architect shall so instruct.

The architect will write to you within 14[3] days regarding all sub-contractors and suppliers, whether nominated or otherwise.[4]

Yours faithfully

Copies: Architect
          Quantity surveyor

---

[1] *Substitute '7.1' when using IFC 84*
[2] *Substitute 'clause 7.4' when using IFC 84*
[3] *Substitute '7' when using IFC 84*
[4] *Omit last four words when using IFC 84*

99   Letter from employer to contractor determining employment after loss or damage

This letter is not suitable for use with MW 80

REGISTERED POST/RECORDED DELIVERY *[as appropriate]*

Dear Sir

[insert appropriate heading]

I refer to your notice of *[insert date]* giving notice of loss or damage occasioned by *[insert particulars of loss or damage which must have been occasioned by one or more of the risks covered by clause 22C.2, or if using IFC 84 clause 6.3C.3]*.

In accordance with clause 22C.4.3.1[1] take this as notice that I hereby forthwith determine your employment under the contract because I consider that it is just and equitable so to do. The rights and duties of the parties are governed by clause 22C.4.3.2.[2]

Yours faithfully

Copies: Architect
Quantity surveyor

---

[1]   *Substitute '6.3C.4.3' when using IFC 84*
[2]   *Substitute '6.3C.4.3' when using IFC 84*

100   **Letter from employer to contractor determining employment**

This letter is suitable only for use with MW 80

REGISTERED POST/RECORDED DELIVERY *[as appropriate]*

Dear Sir

[insert appropriate heading]

In accordance with clause 7.2.1 of the conditions of contract take this as notice that I hereby forthwith determine your employment under this contract without prejudice to any other rights and remedies which I may possess.

You must immediately give up possession of the site of the works.

Take note that I am not bound to make any further payments to you until after completion of the works. I reserve any rights to that time.

Yours faithfully

Copy: Architect

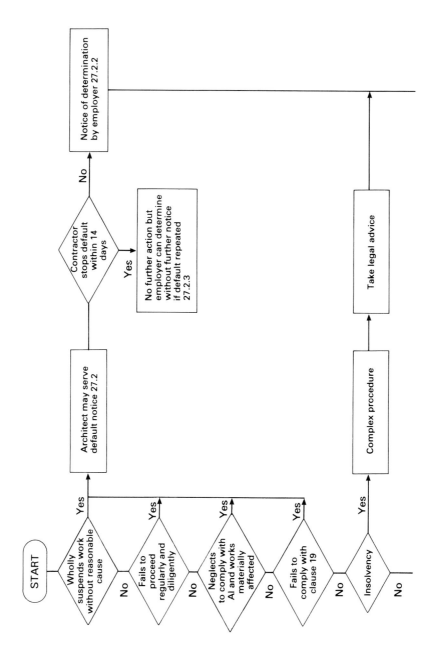

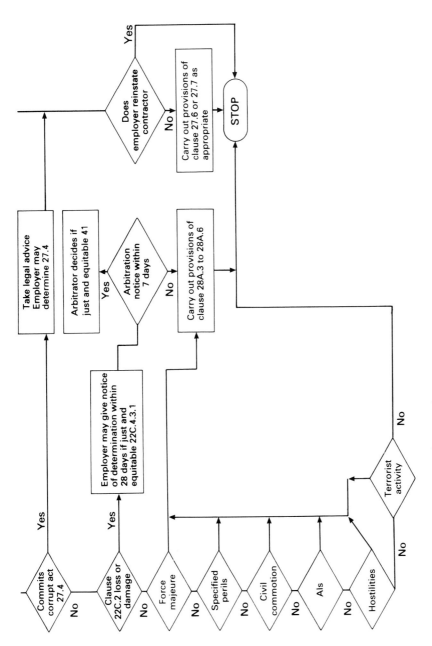

Flowchart 3   Determination by employer under JCT 80.

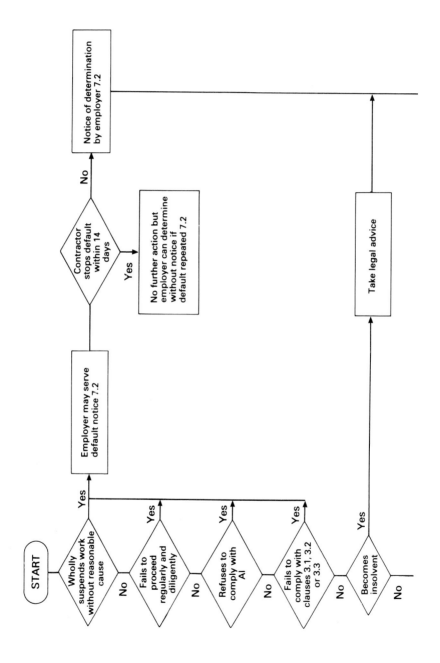

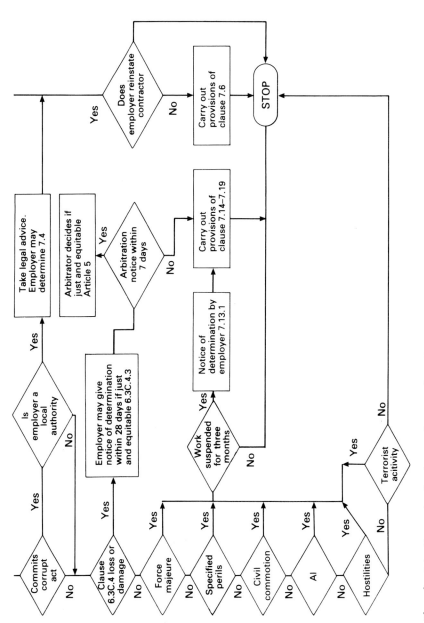

Flowchart 4 Determination by employer under IFC 84.

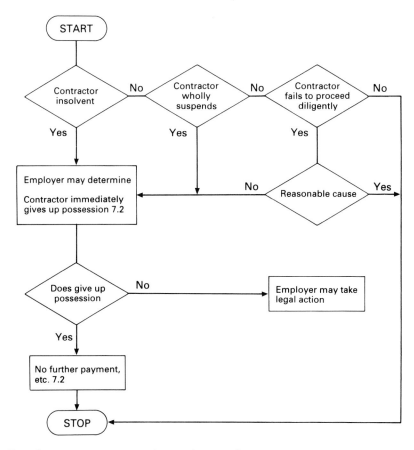

Flowchart 5 Determination by employer under MW 80.

employer to send within ten days by registered post or recorded delivery to determine forthwith the contractor's employment **(98)**.

Note that a repetition of the default at any time after the original notice entitles the employer to determine forthwith without a further 14 days notice.

Clause 27.2.4 requires that the notice shall not be given unreasonably or vexatiously. Although your previous conduct may show that vexation is absent, it is very difficult to decide what reasonable is intended to be. It might very much depend on particular circumstances surrounding the giving of notice.

Consider the four grounds very carefully before giving notice:

❑ *Wholly suspending the works without reasonable cause*
This means the contractor stops all work and, upon your enquiry, fails to give a sufficient reason. A sufficient reason might be, under certain

circumstances, one of the relevant events noted in clause 25.4. You alone will be in a position to decide.

❏ *Failing to proceed regularly and diligently*
The contractor must proceed both regularly *and* diligently. He must have enough resources on site to enable him to make regular daily progress so as to hit any target dates in the contract. His progress must be continuous, industrious and efficient with regard to time, sequence and quality of work.

❏ *Refusing or neglecting to comply with a written notice requiring him to remove defective work or improper materials or goods and thereby the works being materially affected*
Since this situation can normally be dealt with under clause 4.1 (as we have already seen) determination appears to be the last resort if a potentially disastrous situation is developing.

❏ *Failing to comply with clause 19*
Although determination could well be appropriate for a serious breach such as assignment without consent, it seems to be the last resort for the lesser breach of subletting without consent.

The last two grounds for determination under this clause can be summarised as:

❏ The contractor becoming insolvent
❏ The contractor being guilty of a corrupt act

In both cases the complexities are such that legal advice should be sought.

Procedure after determination

After determination, the procedure is clearly laid down in clause 27.6, and there is provision for the employer to allow the contractor to resume work if it is thought desirable in the light of events. The contractor is bound to allow the use of all his plant, goods and materials on site and, except in the case of certain insolvency events, allow the employer the benefit of any agreements with sub-contractors and suppliers. The contractor then has to wait until the completion of the work and all the final costs have been calculated, including any additional loss and expense to the employer. You must not be hurried into arriving at the final figure and, of course, you must work closely with the quantity surveyor. You need not certify any money to the contractor until you are completely satisfied that the employer (the injured party) has been placed in the position, as far as money can do it, he would have been in had the contractor's default and subsequent determination not taken place. The employer has six months from the date of determination to decide whether to complete the project. If he decides that he does not want to complete, an account must be taken to decide the amount owing to the contractor (if any).

Clause 28A sets out six grounds on which either party may determine the contractor's employment. No period of notice is required, but the grounds must have caused suspension of the works for a continuous period of the length noted in the appendix. The grounds are:

- ❑ Force majeure
- ❑ Loss or damage to the works caused by specific perils
- ❑ Civil commotion
- ❑ Architect's instructions issued as a result of the negligence or default of a local authority or statutory undertaker
- ❑ Hostilities involving the UK
- ❑ Terrorist activity

Notice of determination may be given forthwith, but it must not be given vexatiously or unreasonably. The grounds can be roughly classified as neutral, i.e. the fault of neither employer nor contractor.

❑ *Force majeure*
The meaning of this term is somewhat obscure. It is wider than Act of God and refers to circumstances beyond the parties' power to control. A war, a strike or fire caused by lightning are examples of force majeure.

❑ *Loss or damage to the works caused by specified perils*
This is self-explanatory, but the clause excludes the contractor's right to determine under this provision if the loss or damage was caused by negligence of the contractor, his servants or agents or anyone else employed on the works other than the employer, his men or local authority or statutory undertaking carrying out work in pursuance of their statutory duties. So, for example, the contractor may not determine if the loss or damage was caused by a statutory authority carrying out work which was not in pursuance of its statutory duties.

❑ *Civil commotion*
This is a situation which falls between riot and civil war. There must be turbulence or tumult present and it may amount to force majeure.

❏ *Architect's instructions*

Clearly, architect's instructions issued in these circumstances and which cause a long suspension of work cannot be laid at the door of either employer or contractor.

❏ *Hostilities*

This is a state of armed conflict. War may not be declared.

❏ *Terrorist activity*

Regrettably, this needs no explanation.

The procedure after determination is the same as if the contractor determined under clause 28 (see section K26), except that he is not entitled to claim loss and/or expense.

Determination under clause 22C.4.3 is open to either party:

❏ If the contract is for alterations or extensions to existing structures; *and*
❏ loss or damage by one of the risks, covered by the joint names policy for all risks, has affected work carried out or materials on site; *and*
❏ it is just and equitable to do so; *and*
❏ notice is given within 28 days of the occurrence of the loss or damage.

The question is, of course, when will it be just and equitable to serve notice of determination after loss or damage? A situation which would undoubtedly qualify would be if the damage was so considerable as to effectively destroy not only the executed works, but also the existing structure. Each situation must be judged on its merits and if the extent of damage makes continuance of the contract impracticable, notice can probably be served **(99)**. The party receiving the notice has seven days in which to refer the matter to arbitration.

The consequence of determination under this clause is the same as determination under clause 28A.

IFC 84

The procedure is indicated by **Flowchart 4**.

Determination by the employer is governed by clauses 7.1, 7.2, 7.3, 7.4, 7.5, 7.6 and 6.3C.4. The provisions are similar although not identical to the JCT 80 provisions and the above comments are generally applicable.

MW 80

Although the general remarks in this section regarding determination are applicable, the grounds and detailed procedure are different. **Flowchart 5** is applicable. Letters **97**, **98** and **99** are not applicable. Under this contract only two grounds for determination are recognised. The contractor:

❏ Failing to proceed regularly and diligently with the works or wholly suspending the carrying out of the works before completion
❏ The contractor becoming insolvent or making an arrangement with his creditors

As with JCT 80, the first ground requires you to use your careful judgment and the second ground is so complex that legal advice should be obtained.

No period of notice is required in either case, simply service by registered post or recorded delivery of a notice determining the employment of the contractor under the contract **(100)**. The contractor must immediately vacate the site and the employer need make no further payment until after the completion of the works.

In view of the limited remedies available under the contract the employer may be wiser, if the circumstances so justify, to bring the contract to an end by treating the contractor's actions as repudiatory breach. All the common law remedies in damages would then be available. Legal advice must first be sought because neither ground listed in the contract would qualify as repudiatory breach. Suspension, for example, suggests resumption at some future date. The contractor must have shown his intention not to be bound by the contract.

K26 Determination: by contractor (101), (102), (103), (104)

If the contractor successfully determines his employment under clause 28, the results will be disastrous to the employer.

It is essential that, if the contractor purports to determine his employment, you apply all your energies to averting the crisis. The best thing to do is to take the employer along to obtain specialist contractual advice without delay. If you decide not to do that, there are certain things you can do yourself.

The *grounds* for the contractor to determine fall into three quite distinct categories. The *first ground*, quite properly, protects the contractor's right to be paid on time. If the employer gets such a notice, he

101 Letter from architect to employer if attempting to interfere with a certificate

This letter is not suitable for use with MW 80

Dear Sir

[*insert appropriate heading*]

Thank you for your letter of [*insert date*]. My comments are as follows:

The contract imposes on me the obligation to issue all certificates at the appropriate time and to use my professional judgment in so doing.

Clause 28.2.1.2[1] of the conditions of contract gives the contractor power to determine his employment if you interfere with or obstruct the issue of any certificate. The consequences of such determination would be disastrous to the contract.

Naturally, I will bear the legitimate interests of both parties in mind in any decision regarding the issue of certificates.

Yours faithfully

---

[1] *Substitute '7.9.1(b)' when using IFC 84*

102   Letter from employer to contractor if premature determination

REGISTERED POST/RECORDED DELIVERY [*as appropriate*]

Dear Sir

[*insert appropriate heading*]

I am in receipt of your notice dated [*insert date*] purporting to determine the contract under clause 28.2.3[1] of the contract.

Your original notice of default was received on [*insert date*]. The Post Office will be able to confirm to you the date of delivery. Your notice of determination was, therefore, premature and of no effect. You should already have received my cheque in settlement of certificate number [*insert number*] dated [*insert date*] and, unless I hear to the contrary from you, I will assume that you intend to continue work on this contract in the normal way.

Yours faithfully

Copy: Architect

---

[1] *Substitute '7.9.3' when using IFC 84*
     Substitute '7.3' when using MW 80

103 Letter from architect (or employer drafted by architect) to contractor if determination notice issued in accordance with clause 28.2 of JCT 80, clause 7.9.3 of IFC or clause 7.3.1 of MW 80

Dear Sir

[*insert appropriate heading*]

I am in receipt of your notice dated [*insert date*] purporting to determine your employment under the contract.

I consider that you have no valid grounds for determination and your action amounts to a repudiation of the contract for which the employer/I [*as appropriate*] can obtain substantial damages.

It is obviously desirable to continue the contract without recourse to arbitration or litigation and I suggest that you should write a letter withdrawing your notice of determination.

A meeting to discuss your problems would be helpful and I/the architect [*as appropriate*] will telephone you tomorrow to arrange a meeting of all parties.

Yours faithfully

Copy: Employer/architect [*as appropriate*]

104 Letter from architect to contractor confirming agreement after contractor's determination

Dear Sir

[*insert appropriate heading*]

The employer has instructed me to write to you and to refer to the meeting held at [*insert time*] on [*insert date*] at which [*name of contractor's representative*] were present. The following was agreed:

1   [*Note briefly whatever was agreed regarding the contractor's grievances.*]

2   In consideration of you sending the employer a letter withdrawing your notice of determination and resuming work on site within seven days of the above-mentioned meeting, the employer will issue a cheque to you in the agreed sum of [*insert sum*].

Yours faithfully

Copies: Employer
          Quantity surveyor

should pay at once (see item K12). The first three paragraphs of standard letter **67** are appropriate.

The really dangerous aspect is that the first ground is the only one which requires the contractor to give any notice of his intention to determine.

The *second ground* provides that the contractor can determine his employment if 'the employer interferes with or obstructs the issue of any certificate due' under the contract (clause 28.2.1.2). Two points are noteworthy:

❏ The clause does not refer to financial certificates only. You are responsible for the issue of many other certificates, e.g. practical completion, contractor's failure to complete works by completion date, making good of defects, etc. It is important that you issue all certificates at the right time.
❏ Interference or obstruction by the employer will be difficult for the contractor to prove because, if it has occurred, it will usually be between the employer and yourself. However, if it came to arbitration the employer may not be able to claim normal privilege for such letters which go to the root of the allegation. It should be unnecessary to add that you must resist any attempt by the employer to prevent issue of a certificate **(101)**.

The *third ground* permits determination if the employer does not comply with clause 19 (assignment).

In any letter to the contractor you must beware of mentioning the views of the employer in respect of the issue of certificates.

The *fourth ground* is any one of a number of events causing suspension of the work for a continuous period of the length cited in the appendix.

If the contractor issues his notice of determination before the 14 days have expired, he immediately ruins his own case. The situation does sometimes arise as a combination of a postal delay in receiving the original notice and the contractor's anxiety to determine his employment as soon as possible. You should draft a letter for the employer to send **(102)**.

Each event is subject to interpretation. The only relief for the employer is that the contractor would have to be absolutely sure of his facts, with solid supporting evidence, in order to make his determination stick. In order to deflect the contractor, you would have to do some speedy research to build up a contrary argument **(103)**. The contractor may also determine without notice for insolvency. Contractual procedures will be the least of your worries in such circumstances.

If you are unsuccessful in persuading the contractor to withdraw his notice, you must advise the employer that appropriate specialist contractual advice is necessary without delay.

If the contractor's determination is deemed to be good, the consequences to the employer are grave. The contractor is entitled to be paid:

- ❏ The total value of work on the contract fully or partly completed
- ❏ Sums ascertained as loss and/or expense
- ❏ Cost of materials or goods ordered for the works for which the contractor has paid or is bound to pay (the materials or goods then become the property of the employer)
- ❏ Contractor's costs in removing all his plant, tools and temporary buildings under clause 28.4.1
- ❏ Direct loss and/or damage caused to the contractor or any nominated sub-contractor (this will include loss of profit)

The employer will be obliged to invite tenders (inevitably at increased costs) for the completion of the works, and delay will be unavoidable as well as increased professional fees.

If it is decided that there is no defence to the contractor's determination, it is suggested that you take the following immediate course of action:

- ❏ Ask the quantity surveyor to make an immediate estimate of the probable extra cost to the employer, taking everything into account
- ❏ Arrange a meeting between contractor, employer, quantity surveyor and yourself

Your aim should be to ensure that the works are completed as quickly as possible at the least extra cost. Items you will discuss are:

- ❏ The contractor's grievances and what can be done about them
- ❏ The payment of a lump sum in consideration of the contractor agreeing to carry on with the work
- ❏ The withdrawal of the contractor's notice of determination and immediate resumption of work

On the reasonable assumption that the contractor will be content to collect a modest sum without fuss rather than go through the trauma and uncertainty of carrying the determination to completion, agreement should be reached. The agreement, of course, is quite separate from the building contract and it must be settled between employer and contractor. You must waste no time in confirming such agreement **(104)**.

Either party can determine under clauses 28A or 22C.4.3 (see K25).

IFC 84

The grounds for determination are similar to those in JCT 80.

MW 80

Clause 7.3 provides for determination by the contractor on any of four grounds:

- ❑ If the employer fails to make progress payments within 14 days of the due date
- ❑ If the employer or other person for whom he is responsible interferes with the carrying out of the works or fails to make the premises available on the commencement date
- ❑ If the employer suspends carrying out the works for a continuous period of at least one month
- ❑ If the employer becomes insolvent or makes an arrangement with his creditors, etc.

With the exception of the last ground, the contractor cannot determine unless the default is continued for seven days after receipt by registered post or recorded delivery of a notice from the contractor specifying the default. The contractor is entitled to be paid:

- ❑ The value of the work begun and executed
- ❑ Value of materials on site
- ❑ Contractor's costs in removing all temporary buildings, plant, tools and equipment
- ❑ Any direct loss and/or damage caused to the contractor by the determination

Although there is no provision for direct loss and/or damage, the contractor could still bring in action to recover at common law.

Bearing the above points in mind, the remarks in this section, regarding the serious consequences for the employer, are still applicable as are letters **101**, **103** and **104**.

K27 Works by employer or persons employed or engaged by employer: contractor claiming that timing not convenient (105), (106)

The contractor may claim that the timing of work to be carried out by persons engaged by the employer is inconvenient. He may be unwilling to allow them on site and threaten a claim for loss and/or expense

105   Letter from architect to contractor regarding work by employer if information is in the contract bills (or specification)

This letter is not suitable for use with MW 80

Dear Sir

[*insert appropriate heading*]

I refer to your letter of [*insert date*].

Item [*insert page and item number*] of the contract bills/specification [*if applicable*] clearly states that [*describe works*] are to be carried out by the employer. You included the work in your programme submitted to me on [*insert date*].

You have an obligation under clause 29.1[1] to allow [*insert names of persons engaged by the employer*] to carry out their work at the appropriate time, which would appear to be [*insert date*]. Obviously, the employer wishes to assist you as much as possible but that must be balanced against the necessity for him to arrange for his own work. Probably the best solution would be for you to let me know of a date convenient to you as near as possible to the date in your programme and I will see if the employer will agree.

[*Add, if claim is threatened:*]

No claim under clause 26.2.4.1[2] can be entertained unless all the requirements of clause 26[3] are satisfied. It would seem, at this stage, that the employer would have the stronger claim if you were to persist in your reluctance to allow his employees on site.

Yours faithfully

---

[1]   *Substitute '3.11' when using IFC 84*
[2]   *Substitute '4.12.3' when using IFC 84*
[3]   *Substitute '4.11' when using IFC 84*

106 Letter from architect to contractor regarding work by employer if information is not in the contract bills (or specification)

This letter is not suitable for use with MW 80

Dear Sir

[*insert appropriate heading*]

I refer to your letter of [*insert date*] in which you expressed your reluctance to allow the employer to execute [*describe work*] on [*insert date*].

I am surprised by your unhelpful attitude which threatens, over a relatively minor matter, to disrupt the good working relationship we have established on this contract.

Clause 29.2[1] requires your consent to the execution of the work but this consent is something you should not unreasonably withhold. Please let me know by return why the date(s) proposed is (are) not convenient and which date(s) would be convenient so that I can decide whether you are withholding your consent unreasonably. There must be an element of accommodation in every contract and I trust that I am not misguided in my confidence that this matter can be settled in a spirit of mutual co-operation.

[*Add the following if a claim is threatened:*]

Any claim under clause 26[2] will be considered at the appropriate time if it is submitted in the proper form.

Yours faithfully

---

[1] *Substitute '3.11' when using IFC 84*
[2] *Substitute '4.11' when using IFC 84*

under clause 26.2.4.1. A common example of this is when the employer engages his own landscapers or persons to construct and fit plaques, sculptures, etc.

The contractual position can be found in clause 29.

Either the necessary information is provided in the contract bills (or specification) and the contractor should have provided for the work in his programme (letter **105**), or the necessary information is not provided in the contract bills (or specification) and the contractor must not unreasonably refuse to allow the employer to do the work (letter **106**).

IFC 84

A very similar provision is found in this contract in clause 3.11.

MW 80

There is no equivalent provision in this contract.

K28 Reference to 'your' nominated sub-contractor (107)

After nomination, the contractor enters into a contractual relationship with the sub-contractor. You still have certain responsibilities with regard to the sub-contractor in respect of consenting to extensions of time, certifying practical completion, renomination etc, but the situation is entirely different from that which exists if the employer directly employs persons to carry out work. It is, however, very common for a contractor to telephone or write complaining that 'your' nominated sub-contractor is holding up the works for some reason and what do you intend to do about it? Unless the circumstances warrant your direct intervention, which probably means that determination is imminent, you should take no action, but send a fairly brief reply **(107)**.

IFC 84

There are no nominated sub-contractors under this form, but there are named persons as sub-contractors which are similar in that you name them and the contractor enters into a sub-contract with them. The situations in which the contract expects you to take action are more restricted than when dealing with nominated sub-contractors under JCT 80.

107 Letter from architect to contractor if 'your' nominated sub-contractor alleged

This letter is not suitable for use with MW 80

Dear Sir

[*insert appropriate heading*]

Thank you for your letter of [*insert date*].

The circumstances in which I am expected to perform a duty in regard to a nominated sub-contractor[1] are clearly defined in the conditions of contract. You have a contractual relationship with the nominated sub-contractor[1] in question and you should look to the terms of that sub-contract for your remedies in this instance.

Yours faithfully

---

[1] *Substitute 'named person' when using IFC 84*

MW 80

There are no nominated or named sub-contractors under this form, therefore the situation should not arise.

K29 Late evidence of payment of nominated sub-contractors provided by the main contractor (108)

The main contractor may have failed to provide reasonable proof of payment to a nominated sub-contractor under clause 35.13.5, and the employer, therefore, paid the nominated sub-contractor directly, reducing future payment to the main contractor accordingly. If, at a very late stage in the contract, the main contractor produces proof that he did pay the nominated sub-contractor, what should you do?

You should let the main and nominated sub-contractor sort it out between themselves.

IFC 84

There is no equivalent provision under this form.

MW 80

There is no provision for the nomination of sub-contractors or suppliers.

K30 Nominated sub-contractor: extension of time (109), (110), (111)

The provisions for extension of time to nominated sub-contractors and certification for failure to complete on time are fraught with complexities which are best illustrated by an example. In order to gain some financial advantage, the contractor may request you to give written consent for extension of time to a nominated sub-contractor which you decide, having studied the facts, is far too short, putting an unfair burden on the nominated sub-contractor. You must, therefore, withhold your consent **(109)**.

The contractor will undoubtedly ask you to fix the length of extension. Beware of doing this. It is the contractor's responsibility and

108 Letter from architect to contractor if late proof of payment of nominated sub-contractor produced

This letter is only suitable for use with JCT 80

Dear Sir

[*insert appropriate heading*]

Thank you for your letter of [*insert date*].

The employer has discharged his obligations to the nominated sub-contractor and yourself under the provisions of clause 35.13. His action was taken strictly in accordance with the contract provisions as a result of your failure to provide proof of payment.

I suggest that you take the matter up with your sub-contractor.

Yours faithfully

Copy: Quantity surveyor

109   Letter from architect to contractor withholding consent to extension of time to nominated sub-contractor

This letter is only suitable for use with JCT 80

Dear Sir

[*insert appropriate heading*]

Thank you for your letter of [*insert date*].

I cannot give my consent to your proposed award of extension of time because I consider the period of time is not correct.

Yours faithfully

110 Letter from architect to contractor declining to fix period of extension of time for nominated sub-contractor

This letter is only suitable for use with JCT 80

Dear Sir

[*insert appropriate heading*]

Thank you for your letter of [*insert date*].

It is your responsibility to fix the period of extension of time for the nominated sub-contractor under clause 35.14. My duty is to give or withhold my consent.

Yours faithfully

111 Letter from architect to contractor if he demands certificate under clause 35.15.1

This letter is only suitable for use with JCT 80

Dear Sir

[*insert appropriate heading*]

Thank you for your letter of [*insert date*].

Clause 35.15.1 requires me to certify that the nominated sub-contractor has failed to complete the sub-contract work within the period specified in the sub-contract provided that he has so failed and that I am satisfied that the provisions of clause 35.14 have been properly applied. I am not so satisfied and until the provisions are applied to my satisfaction, I decline to certify as you request.

Yours faithfully

money is at stake for which the aggrieved party may try to hold you responsible **(110)**.

The contractor may then submit a more realistic period of extension to which you can consent. He may, however, demand that you issue a certificate that the nominated sub-contractor has failed to complete within the period specified in the nominated sub-contract. This ploy can and should be countered **(111)** so that the contractor is forced to submit a proper extension for your consideration.

IFC 84

There is no equivalent provision in this form.

MW 80

There is no provision for the nomination of sub-contractors.

K31 Nominated sub-contractor: drawings for approval (112)

The contractor will usually submit drawings received from the nominated sub-contractor or supplier for your approval. On the basis that they are not design drawings, but simply produced from your own drawings, it is the contractor's responsibility to check and co-ordinate them. A typical example is a window schedule or a setting out drawing for a staircase balustrade. You must be careful not to relieve the contractor of his responsibility. The situation is different if the drawings have some design content which is normally part of your design responsibility.

If the nominated sub-contractor has supplied his drawings directly to you under the employer/nominated sub-contractor form of agreement, this type of letter is not really suitable, and it is then up to you to check the details for incorporation in your own drawings.

IFC 84

The remarks in this section are applicable to drawings produced by named persons as sub-contractors.

MW 80

There is no provision for nominating sub-contractors. The remarks in

112 Letter from architect to contractor if drawings submitted for approval

Dear Sir

[*insert appropriate heading*]

Thank you for your letter of [*insert date*] enclosing two copies of [*insert name of sub-contractor*][1] drawings numbers [*insert drawing numbers*].

My comments are as follows:

[*List comments*]

It is your responsibility under the contract to check and co-ordinate these sub-contractors' drawings required to execute the works. This letter must not be construed so as to relieve you of that responsibility and my comments are so restricted. I have retained one copy of the drawings for my records.

Yours faithfully

---

[1] *Omit when using MW 80*

this section are generally applicable to the rare instances where the contractor sends you a drawing for approval. Letter **112** is applicable with the amendments shown.

K32 Arbitration: threatened over a small matter (113), (114)

If the contractor does not agree with your decision in some respect, he may write to the employer to ask him to concur in the appointment of an arbitrator. It may simply be a threat to persuade you to alter your decision. What you should do next depends upon:

- Whether the item is paltry in financial terms (depends upon value of the item in dispute in relation to the whole contract and the resources of the contractor) **(113)**
- Whether, irrespective of the value of the item, your knowledge of the contractor leads you to believe that he will proceed to arbitration **(114)**. Take care with this assessment and be pessimistic

Points to note:

- It is thought by some that if the employer concurs in the appointment of an arbitrator, this may tend to give the impression that he thinks there is some merit in the contractor's case. On the other hand, the employer's prompt agreement may give pause for thought to a contractor who is simply trying to threaten
- Always try to sort out the difference by a meeting
- Most projected arbitrations peter out or are settled before the actual hearing stage is reached
- The outcome of arbitration, like the outcome of litigation, never can be predicted by either party, no matter how strong they consider their case to be

K33 Client: instructions given direct to the contractor (115), (116), (117), (118)

Usually the architect would prefer his client to stay away from the site until the works have reached practical completion. A client on site tends to be like a patient supervising the removal of his own appendix; this is particularly true of professional clients. However, many clients make a practice of visiting the site. If your client does this, always accompany him. Make sure, before the commencement of the work on

113   Letter from architect to contractor if item is paltry or architect does not consider that he intends to proceed to arbitration

REGISTERED POST/RECORDED DELIVERY [*as appropriate*]

Dear Sir

[*insert appropriate heading*]

I am in receipt of your letter of [*insert date*]. [*If sent to the employer, add: 'passed to me by the employer'.*]

The step you propose is very serious and tends to be expensive to both sides irrespective of the outcome. Indeed, in the present case the legal and other costs are likely to outweigh any financial advantage many times over. Naturally, I am confident that my decision would be upheld by an arbitration. Nevertheless, none of us, as reasonable people, would relish the idea of many months of additional work and expense if it can be avoided.

Perhaps the next step should be a meeting at this office as soon as possible in an attempt to resolve this dispute. If this idea is of interest, please confirm in writing that you withdraw your notice requiring concurrence to enable the meeting to proceed in an appropriate atmosphere.

Yours faithfully

Copy: Employer

114 Letter from architect to contractor if it is believed that he intends to take the matter to arbitration

REGISTERED POST/RECORDED DELIVERY [*as appropriate*]

Dear Sir

[*insert appropriate heading*]

I am in receipt of your letter of [*insert date*]. [*If sent to the employer, add: 'passed to me by the employer'.*]

The step you propose is serious with severe financial implications as to costs for both parties. I firmly hold that my decision, which you seek to question, is correct.

Before I advise the employer regarding the appointment of an arbitrator, I suggest we meet at my office to discuss your problems like reasonable people. If you wish to do that, please telephone me to arrange a convenient time and confirm in writing by return that you will suspend the operation of the arbitration notice for a period of say four weeks from the date of your letter.

Yours faithfully

Copy: Employer

115 Letter from architect to client warning against direct contact with the contractor

Dear Sir

[*insert appropriate heading*]

May I offer a word of advice regarding your relations with the contractor?

I have the duty to administer all aspects of the above works in accordance with the contract you have signed. If the contractor communicates with you by letter, telephone or personal visit, please refer him to me and let me know immediately. It is not advisable for you to answer any of his queries or make any decisions regarding the contract without consulting me. This could also be costly. If there are any matters requiring your decision, I will refer them, as they arise, to you with any observations I may have.

I understand that you may wish to visit the site to see the work in progress from time to time. If so, please let me know so that I can make myself available to accompany you on each occasion to take care of any points which may arise.

Yours faithfully

116 Letter from architect to client regarding client's instructions on site

Dear Sir

[*insert appropriate heading*]

When I called on site today, the contractor informed me that you had preceded me and given him the following instructions:

[*Insert instructions issued by your client.*]

Your instructions have already been put into effect with the result that [*summarise the material consequences*].

Naturally, the contractor will claim appropriate payments, and I have informed him that he must send such claim directly to you as strictly it is outside the contract.

It would be in your own best interests for you to visit the site only in my company so that you have professional advice for any amendments you may wish to make.

Yours faithfully

Copy: Quantity surveyor

117   Letter from architect to client if asked to retrieve the situation

Dear Sir

[*insert appropriate heading*]

I refer to our recent conversation regarding the alleged instructions which I mentioned in my letter of [*insert date of your previous letters*].

I note that you wish me to retrieve the situation as far as possible and, naturally, I wish to do anything I can to assist. I will proceed on the understanding that you accept that I have no responsibility for the consequences of the alleged instruction nor the consequences of my attempts to retrieve the matter. The contractor could argue:

1   that you varied the terms of the contract;
2   that your alleged instructions were outside the contract altogether and amounted to another contract.

How far he would succeed in his contentions could be a matter for a court to decide.

Yours faithfully

118   Letter from architect to contractor regarding employer's alleged instructions

Dear Sir

[*insert appropriate heading*]

I refer to my visit to site on [*insert date*] when you informed me that you had [*insert variation carried out*] in response to a direct instruction from the employer.

[*Insert one of the following sentences as appropriate:*]

My client informs me that he did not give you instructions during his visit to site or at any other time.

[*or*]

My client informs me that he asked you to seek confirmation from me before carrying out any additional work in accordance with his suggestions.

The conditions of contract provide that all instructions must be issued by me. You are, therefore, in breach of contract. Are you prepared to rectify the situation on site so that it is in conformity with the contract without the necessity for an instruction under clause 8.4[1]?

Yours faithfully

Copies: Employer
         Quantity surveyor

---

[1]   *Substitute '3.14' when using IFC 84*
     Omit when using MW 80

site, that you warn your client of the problems which might arise if he has direct contact with the contractor. Your letter **(115)** could form part of another letter which you are writing about other aspects of the contract.

Despite the warning, your client may visit the site without you. What is worse, he may give an instruction or answer a query which the contractor puts into effect without consulting you. The position is very awkward. Although you alone are empowered to issue instructions (clause 4) under the contract, it is clear that the two parties to a contract, by mutual agreement, can vary any of the terms at any time. In effect, it could mean that the contractor can proceed on instructions from the employer (your client) and claim payment.

Your relationship with your client is a very delicate and personal thing and you must adjust your letter **(116)** accordingly.

There may be no problem, because your client may be prepared to stand by his instruction and pay the contractor directly, or to authorise you to ratify it with an architect's instruction so that it can be paid for under the contract. However, it is possible that when your client realises the full extent of the consequences of his direct instructions, he will ask you to retrieve the situation for him. He may possibly say that he asked the contractor to consult you before carrying out his instructions or that he never gave any instructions at all. The employer and contractor are now in a potential 'dispute situation'. It is a situation not of your making. Indeed you have done your best to avoid it. It is not your problem but, to preserve your relations with your client, you will be anxious to try and help. Tread carefully and send a preliminary letter **(117)** to your client before seeing what you can do with the contractor **(118)**.

The contractor basically can only answer yes or no. If yes, there should be no further problems. If no, you must involve your client fully. He got himself into the mess by visiting the site. You will probably advise him bearing in mind that:

❏ If you issue an instruction in accordance with clause 8.4 to remove defective work, the contractor may seek arbitration or litigation
❏ The chances are that the hearing would support the instruction under clause 8.4, but this is by no means certain because much would turn upon the precise facts of the case as found by the arbitrator or the judge
❏ Your duty under the contract is to issue the clause 8.4 instruction

You should encourage your client to take appropriate legal advice at this stage and you should protect yourself by obtaining his precise written instructions on the matter.

IFC 84

Clause 3.5 empowers you to issue instructions. Instructions to remove defective work would be under 3.14.

MW 80

All instructions are empowered by clause 3.5.

K34 Client: additional items forgotten by architect (119)

In almost every contract it is inevitable that you will have overlooked some items at tender stage. You will be involved in issuing instructions to correct the situation.

The client will not always appreciate that some items will be forgotten. It is prudent to seek his approval for what might be termed 'legitimate' extras as they occur (such as items necessitated by his own changes of mind or unexpected additional expense due to unavailability of material etc.). Items which have been forgotten may be embarrassing, but you must refer back to your client for authority to expend money. If you adopt a straightforward approach, you should have no difficulty provided that they are not so expensive that they would have pushed the original tender price into the prohibitive bracket had they been included at tender stage **(119)**.

K35 Clerk of works: faulty written directions acted upon by the contractor (120)

Although the clerk of works has no power to issue instructions, he will frequently issue directions. Usually, the directions are concerned with the correction of defective workmanship or materials but sometimes the directions take on more of the character of instructions to vary or do additional work. Equally, the contractor falls into the habit of carrying out the directions as though they were architect's instructions. All may be well until the contractor complies with a direction with which you do not agree. If you find yourself in this position there are three points to consider:

❑ The necessity to restore the situation to your satisfaction
❑ The understandable, although unjustified, annoyance of the contractor if considerable expense is involved

119   Letter from architect to employer regarding items forgotten

Dear Sir

[*insert appropriate heading*]

I refer to my brief telephone call of [*insert date*]. I confirm that the following items were not included in the bills of quantities/specification/schedules of work [*as applicable*]:

[*List items not included*]

The items are clearly necessary and I should be pleased to have your authority to instruct the contractor to carry out the work/supply the materials [*as applicable*]. I enclose the latest financial statement from which you can see that

[*Then add either:*]

the inclusion of these items is not likely to result in the contract sum being exceeded if some of the savings achieved in other areas are taken into account.

[*Or:*]

the inclusion of these items is likely to result in the contract sum being exceeded by [*insert amount*], even after savings in other areas are taken into account. Had the items been included at tender stage, of course, the position would be just the same.

Yours faithfully

Copy: Quantity surveyor

120   Letter from architect to contractor regarding clerk of works' direction

Dear Sir

[*insert appropriate heading*]

I enclose my architect's instruction regarding [*describe briefly*].

I regret the necessity of sending such an instruction. However, there is really no alternative. When you complied with the direction of the clerk of works, you were acting in breach of contract, although, no doubt, with the very best of intentions to progress the works as quickly as possible.

Perhaps it is opportune to remind you that the role of the clerk of works is that of inspector and, while he will always attempt to assist you with advice and guidance, he is not empowered to issue instructions. He is, however, a man of considerable experience and I sincerely hope that you will continue to work with him in a spirit of mutual co-operation.

Yours faithfully

Copy: Clerk of works

❏ The need to maintain the future credibility of the clerk of works

The contractor should not carry out clerk of works' directions unless you confirm them. The other two points are tricky if you are to carry on a good relationship with all parties on site. It is presumed that you have been careful to spell out the duties of the clerk of works at the beginning of the contract. You will have done it at the first meeting prior to the commencement of work and had the item properly minuted. So now you must issue an instruction requiring the contractor to remove faulty work from site. With the instruction send a letter **(120)**.

IFC 84

Although there is provision for a clerk of works under this form (clause 3.10), he must not issue directions, not even those which are of no effect as under JCT 80. It may be that he issues directions, of course, even though he is not supposed to do so, and if he does, letter **120** is applicable.

MW 80

There is no provision for a clerk of works in the conditions but you might have made provision, in similar terms to the standard form, in the specification. If so, this section is applicable.

K36 Clerk of works: verification of daywork sheets (121)

It is common practice for the contractor to deliver daywork sheets (referred to as vouchers in the conditions, clause 13.5.4) to the clerk of works for verification, sometimes as much as a month after the work has been carried out. The conditions call for the vouchers to be delivered to the architect or his authorised representative not later than the end of the week following the week in which the work has been carried out.

The clerk of works is not your authorised representative. Vouchers delivered after time need not be verified and thereby the ground is prepared for a lengthy dispute between respective quantity surveyors – something to be avoided if possible. It makes sense to make the clerk of works your authorised representative in a limited capacity for the sole purpose of verifying the vouchers. If you decide to do so, you should inform the contractor at the beginning of the contract.

121   Letter from architect to contractor regarding verification of daywork vouchers

This letter is not suitable for use with MW 80

Dear Sir

[*insert appropriate heading*]

I should be pleased if you would note that the clerk of works, [*insert name*], is my authorised representative for the purpose of <u>clause 13.5.4 of the Conditions,</u>[1] verification of daywork vouchers, and for that purpose alone.

If work is carried out in accordance with clause 13.5.4[2], the vouchers should be delivered to the clerk of works not later than the end of the week following that in which the work has been executed. Vouchers delivered after that time will not be signed.

Please note that the signature of the clerk of works on the vouchers is not an authorisation for payment but only a confirmation that the time, labour, plant and materials noted therein are correct.

Yours faithfully

Copy: Clerk of works
         Quantity surveyor

---

[1]   *Omit underlined portion when using IFC 84*
[2]   *Substitute '3.7.5' when using IFC 84*

IFC 84

There is provision for dayworks in clause 3.7.5, but not for vouchers. There will be a need for them if dayworks are authorised, and a need for prompt checking. This letter will be applicable in those circumstances.

MW 80

There is no provision for daywork sheets in this contract.

K37 Consultants: instructions direct to the contractor (122)

It is common to have consultants employed upon contracts, quantity surveyors, structural and service engineers and landscape artists being the most usual. They frequently visit the site to inspect their own work and often give instructions directly to the person-in-charge or even to the specialist firms themselves.

The contract provides for instructions to be issued by the architect alone. The ideal is for you to accompany the consultants on every site visit so that you can, if you approve, translate their requirements into architects instructions. Their instructions are of no effect otherwise. It is assumed that you will have made the position abundantly clear at the first meeting of all parties before the beginning of the contract. Many consultants adopt the admirable practice of sending any instructions directly to the architect in draft for his approval and issue.

What if, despite your precautions, a consultant does issue instructions directly to the contractor and they are not to your liking? The position is somewhat similar to that of the clerk of works (see K35). You can put matters right by issuing an instruction to remove the work from site. You can do this under clause 8.4. You must, however, write to the contractor and emphasise the position.

IFC 84

The position is identical under this form of contract. You can order removal from site under clause 3.14.

MW 80

It is unusual for a consultant to be employed on this contract, but the section is generally applicable if a consultant is used. Any instruction must be under clause 3.5.

122 Letter from architect to contractor regarding consultant's instructions

Dear Sir

[*insert appropriate heading*]

In view of recent events on site, I am writing to draw your attention to minute number [*insert number*] of the meeting held on [*insert date*].

The contract provides that the architect is the only person empowered to issue instructions. All other instructions, from whatever source, are of no effect unless confirmed by the architect in writing. The restriction applies to all consultants engaged by the employer upon this contract.

If we are to avoid a repetition of the problems recently experienced, you must take care to comply with my instructions only and refer any other instructions, suggestions or directions to me for my decision.

Yours faithfully

Copies: All consultants

K38 Consultants: problems with builder's work (123), (124)

The consultant is responsible for informing you of all his builder's work requirements before quantities are finalised, and you should make sure that you obtain all the work requirements of the consultant in writing or on drawings. It is assumed that the consultant is engaged directly by your client.

As work progresses, minor adjustments should present no problem. If some of the builder's work, constructed in accordance with the consultant's requirements, proves to be quite unsuitable and considerable expense is necessary to correct matters, what is your position? Your client will usually look to you for help.

First, you must resist the temptation to try and make the best of things. Place the responsibility squarely where it belongs – with the consultant. Secondly, if the consultant is unwilling or unable to correct the problem at no additional cost, he must report to your mutual client. Eventually, you may be involved in sorting out the problem, but it is essential that you enter that situation without liability. It is one of the reasons that you have ensured that the consultant is directly employed and that you have taken on the commission on the basis of SFA 92 or CE/95.

In the first instance **(123)** you are really asking the consultant to either devise a method of overcoming the problem without additional cost to the contract, or pay for the additional work himself.

In your second letter **(124)** you are exerting pressure on the consultant and at the same time distancing yourself from the cause of the trouble.

IFC 84 and MW 80

This section is also applicable to these forms of contract.

K39 Extension of time (125), (126), (127), (128) (flowcharts 6, 7)

K39.1 Awarding an extension if bills of quantities show phased completion and only one completion date in contract

Even if the sectional completion supplement is not incorporated in the contract, it is not uncommon for contracts consisting of a number of

123 Letter from architect to consultant if there is a problem with builder's work

Dear Sir

[*insert appropriate heading*]

I refer to the problem on site with regard to [*insert brief details of the problem*].

The builder's work has been carried out strictly in accordance with the details you supplied to me with your letter of [*insert date*]. I should be pleased if you would inform me how the matter can be resolved at no additional cost to the contract. If, as appears likely, it proves impossible to amend the work without additional cost, I request you to report the matter directly to our mutual client, copy to me, and ask for immediate instructions.

[*If the work is urgent add the following paragraph (but not when using MW 80)*]

The work is in danger of being delayed, and, if the contractor makes a claim, I shall have no alternative but to request the quantity surveyor to ascertain the amount of loss and/or expense due to the contractor in accordance with clause 26[1] of the contract.

Yours faithfully

---

[1]   *Substitute '4.11' when using IFC 84*

124 Letter from architect to client if consultant declines to correct problem or report to client

Dear Sir

[*insert appropriate heading*]

A problem has arisen with regard to the [*insert type of consultancy service*].

The builder's work has been constructed strictly in accordance with your consultant's requirements.

I have asked the consultant to report directly to you on the matter and I should be pleased to receive your immediate instructions.

Any delay to the progress of the works due to late instructions will entitle the contractor to claim loss and/or expense.[1]

Yours faithfully

Copy: Consultant

---

[1] *Omit this paragraph when using MW 80*

125   Letter from architect to contractor if he presses for extension of time

Dear Sir

[*insert appropriate heading*]

Thank you for your letter of [*insert date*].

I will make a decision on the matter of any extension of time in accordance with the provisions of the contract.

In my opinion it is not reasonably practicable to do so at this time.

[*Add the following if appropriate, but not when using MW 80:*]

because you have not yet furnished reasonably sufficient particulars and estimate. I require [*insert requirements*] before I can consider the matter further.

Yours faithfully

126 Letter from architect to contractor seeking agreement to extend the review period

This letter is not suitable for use with MW 80

Dear Sir

[*insert appropriate heading*]

Thank you for your letter of [*insert date*].

As you are no doubt aware, my power to carry out a review and make further extensions of time expired on [*insert date*], 12 weeks after the date of practical completion. I would be prepared to reconsider the matter of extending the contract period, but first you would have to agree with the employer a variation to clause 25.3.3[1] enabling me to do so. If you wish me to proceed, all that is required is for you to confirm the same directly to the employer with a copy to me. I will copy him with this letter and he will acknowledge your letter indicating his agreement.

Yours faithfully

Copy: Employer

---

[1]   *Substitute '2.3' when using IFC 84*

127 Letter from architect to contractor if payment requested for using best endeavours

This letter is not suitable for use with MW 80

Dear Sir

[*insert appropriate heading*]

Thank you for your letter of [*insert date*].

I will carefully consider any claim for additional payment if it is properly presented in accordance with the provisions of the contract.

However, you must remember that there is no provision for acceleration in this contract. You must constantly use your best endeavours to prevent delay in the progress of the works in accordance with clause 25.3.4.1.[1] That is all I have requested you to do and, because it is included in the contract, no extra payment is possible.

Yours faithfully

Copy: Quantity surveyor

[1] *Substitute '2.3' when using IFC 84*

128 Letter from architect to contractor if claim rejected

Dear Sir

[insert appropriate heading]

Thank you for your letter of [insert date].

[Add one of the following paragraphs as appropriate.]

Before I can consider your claim for extension of time you must supply me with all the information required by clause 25.2[1] of the conditions.[2]

[or]

I have carefully considered your notice of delay and accompanying particulars and it is my opinion that no extension of time should be given at this time.

Yours faithfully

Copy: Quantity surveyor

---

[1] Substitute 'I require under clause 2.3' for the underlined portion when using IFC 84

[2] This paragraph is not appropriate for use with MW 80

units (housing estates for example) to be treated as for phased completion. This is often done by including a table in the bills of quantities (or specification) showing the various periods by which the units must be complete. For example: 'Blocks A, B and C to be completed within 9, 10 and 11 months respectively of the date for possession'. The completion date in the appendix is often noted as one day only.

In the example noted above, the appendix completion date might be 20 July 1996. This would mean that the employer, in the bills of quantities (or specification), intended Blocks A, B and C to be completed by 20 May, 20 June and 20 July 1996 respectively.

What is the position if an extension of time is requested? Some architects purport to award extensions to the individual block periods. This is wrong (unless separate completion dates are entered in the appendix and several other complicated amendments are made) because:

❑ Where only one completion date is entered it is the completion date for the whole contract (e.g. blocks A, B and C)
❑ Clause 13.1.2.4 refers to restrictions imposed in the contract bills (or specification) in regard to the completion of work in any particular order
❑ Clause 2.2.1 gives precedence to the articles of agreement, conditions and appendix over the contract bills (or specification)

It therefore seems clear that the blocks must be finished in the order A, B, C. However, provided that the contract, as a whole, is completed by the date for completion in the appendix (e.g. 20 July 1996), it appears quite correct if block A is finished on 18 July and block B on 19 July 1996.

If the employer were to attempt to deduct liquidated damages in respect of blocks A and B on the basis of the table in the bills of quantities (or specification), the contractor could argue that those provisions were in conflict with the single completion date in the appendix which must prevail. Even if liquidated damages are expressed as £x per dwelling per week, they are not enforceable. It is meaningless to attempt to award an extension of time in respect of the individual blocks. The moral is that, if the employer requires certain blocks to be completed by specific dates, he should use the sectional completion supplement and enter separate dates in the appendix. This allows each section to be considered individually for such things as possession, completion, extensions of time and liquidated damages.

In the example used above, you would have to consider simply whether the single completion date should be extended. In passing, it would seem that the only real censure the employer possesses, if the blocks are not completed in the correct order, is to take possession only

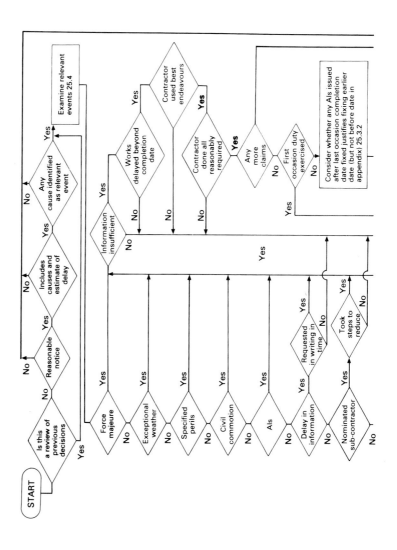

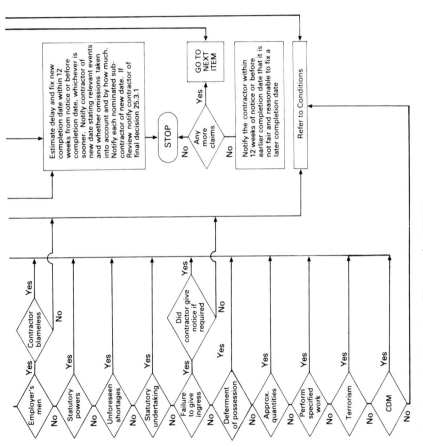

Flowchart 6 Extension of time under JCT 80.

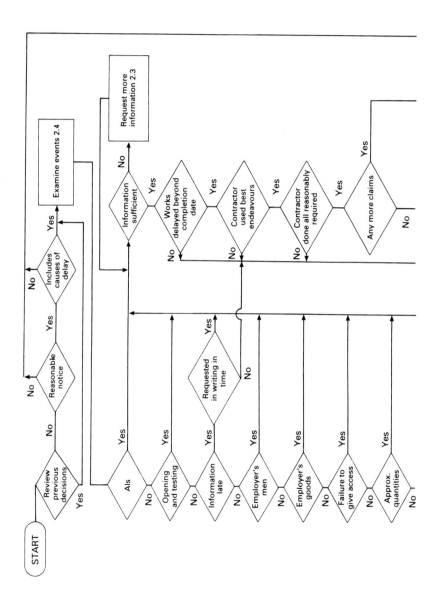

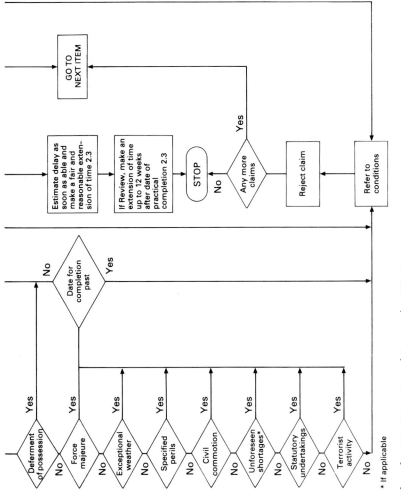

Flowchart 7   Extension of time under IFC 84.

* If applicable

in the order he requires them. So that if block B was completed first, he could refuse to accept it until block A was finished and accepted.

IFC 84

The comments above are generally applicable. Clause 3.6.2 refers to restrictions on the order of the work etc. Clause 1.3 gives precedence to the articles, conditions, supplemental conditions, appendix over the specification (or schedules of work or contract bills). A sectional completion supplement is available for this contract.

MW 80

It is unlikely that phased completion would be used with this contract and, therefore, this section is not applicable.

K39.2 Failure to fix a completion date within the appropriate time (125), (126)

Architects appear to be notorious, among contractors at any rate, for slowness in giving extensions of time. On the face of it, the contract places a strict requirement on the architect, in clauses 25.3.1 and 25.3.3, to fix a completion date within specific time limits, and, obviously, it is important for you to adhere to the time limits. The requirements fall into two distinct parts:

❏ Fixing a new completion date not later than 12 weeks from receipt of notice, reasonably sufficient particulars and estimate or, if the former completion date would occur before the expiry of 12 weeks, before the former completion date expires
❏ Notifying the contractor, not later than 12 weeks after the date of practical completion, that the completion date is confirmed or amended

You may well argue that it is sometimes impossible for you to give the extension within the time limit set down before practical completion. Your problem is taken into account in clause 25.3.1 which requires you to adhere to the time limit only if it is 'reasonably practicable' having regard to the sufficiency of the notice, particulars and estimates received from the contractor. The contractor may not see it this way and may press you for a decision **(125)**.

After practical completion, if you should overlook the duty of notifying the contractor in accordance with clause 25.3.3, you risk the contractor arguing that the completion date, being unconfirmed, is of no effect. If the contractor were able to prove this point, the employer would be unable to recover any liquidated damages for any overrun on the part of the contractor. It would not, of course, prevent the employer attempting to prove actual damage at common law, but that would be a complicated business. You would be in breach of your duty and the employer may look to you for recompense.

Clearly, you should strive to fix the date within the allotted period. If you overlook your duty, it is probable that your power to fix a new date for completion has expired. The very worst position to be in is if you know the contractor is entitled to a greater extension of the contract period, but you are unable to give it. Very often, a contractor will be anxious to obtain a further extension of time, which will be more valuable than arguments about 'time at large' which may need arbitration to settle. It may be worth asking the contractor to extend the 12 week period to enable you to carry out the final review under clause 25.3.3. Any contractual term can be varied if both contractor and employer agree **(126)**.

IFC 84

The comments above are generally applicable but there is no requirement in clause 2.3 for you to grant an extension of time within any particular time limit before completion date – simply to make a fair and reasonable extension of time *so soon as you are able* to estimate the length of delay. After practical completion, you must review extensions of time, as under JCT 80, within 12 weeks and letter **126** is applicable.

MW 80

Provision for extension of time is very brief. There is no time limit set but clearly you must give your decision as soon as possible. If the contractor presses you unreasonably, letter **125** is applicable. There is no provision for a review.

K39.3 Best endeavours: contractor's claim for extra payment (127)

The contractor is required to constantly use his best endeavours in accordance with clause 25.3.4.1. If you are too enthusiastic in your encouragement, the contractor may respond by requesting additional payment.

IFC 84

'Best endeavours' is included in clause 2.3.

MW 80

There is no specific requirement that the contractor should constantly use his best endeavours, although clearly it is something you have to take into account when considering awarding an extension of time, because it is part of the contractor's ordinary duty to mitigate loss. This section is not applicable.

K39.4 Claims for extension of time: procedure (128)

The main steps in considering a claim for extension of time are set out in **Flowchart 6**.

After practical completion is certified, you must take all relevant events into account even though the contractor has given no notice of them. If you reject the contractor's claims, for whatever reason, quite a short letter is indicated. If the contractor asks you why you have not awarded an extension time, you do not have to tell him. Do not give your reasons in writing because:

❏ Consideration of delay is usually too complex to be explained without a lengthy report
❏ Anything you write down may be dissected word by word if the matter eventually goes to arbitration

There is little guidance to be found on the process of estimating extensions of time. Some architects favour tabulating all facts in chronological order with accompanying remarks. Others prefer to work from an annotated master programme in network form. This is the best approach. There are several computer programs which will make light work of entering delays into the programme and reconciling so-called concurrent delays. Do not forget that your award is a fair and reasonable estimate, very seldom a precise thing. In giving your extension you must:

❏ Fix a new completion date
❏ State which relevant events you have taken into account
❏ State the extent, if any, to which you have regard to any instruction requiring the omission of any work issued since the fixing of the last completion date
❏ Notify every nominated sub-contractor

Once again, it is unwise to elaborate on your reasoning.

IFC 84

The above comments are also applicable to this contract. The main steps in considering a claim for extension of time are set out in **Flowchart 7**.

MW 80

The provision for extension of time makes reference to 'reasons beyond the control of the contractor including compliance with any instruction of the architect ... under the contract whose issue is not due to a default of the contractor'. In deciding whether to award an extension you must take into account everything beyond the control of the contractor. Letter **125** and the general remarks in this section are applicable, but note that in any award you should only:

- ❏ Fix a new completion date
- ❏ State briefly the reason for your award, e.g. exceptionally adverse weather conditions

K40 Claims for loss and/or expense: procedure (129), (130), (131), (Flowcharts 8, 9)

The main steps in considering a claim for loss and/or expense are set out in **Flowchart 8**.

There are three basic letters to be sent to the contractor: two if the claim is rejected for various reasons **(129)**, **(130)**, one if the claim is accepted **(131)**. Note that if the contractor is late in making his application, you have no power to consider it. Whether a contractor's application is so late that it cannot be considered is a matter of fact, taking into account all relevant circumstances.

Useful questions to bear in mind in the case of a late application are:

- ❏ Has the late delivery of the claim, by its lateness alone, made your consideration or ascertainment difficult?
- ❏ Is the employer likely to suffer any direct or indirect loss solely attributable to the lateness of the claim?
- ❏ If the contractor had made his application earlier, could you have taken any action which you could not take subsequently, to reduce the loss?

Of course, it is almost certain that the contractor will wish to meet you to discuss some aspects of his claim. Not everything can be done by letter.

129   Letter from architect to contractor if claim rejected due to lack of information

This letter is not suitable for use with MW 80

Dear Sir

[*insert appropriate heading*]

I refer to your claim for loss and/or expense, under clause 26[1] of the conditions, received on [*insert date*].

Before I can give proper consideration to your claim, you must comply with all the provisions of clause 26[1].

You have not provided enough information.

Yours faithfully

Copy: Quantity surveyor

---

[1]   *Substitute '4.11' when using IFC 84*

130 Letter from architect to contractor if claim rejected after consideration of all the evidence

This letter is not suitable for use with MW 80

Dear Sir

[*insert appropriate heading*]

I refer to your claim for loss and/or expense, under clause 26[1] of the conditions, received on [*insert date*].

After careful consideration of the evidence, I have to inform you that I can find no grounds for ascertaining any loss and/or expense at this time.

Yours faithfully

Copy: Quantity surveyor

---

[1] *Substitute '4.11' when using IFC 84*

131   Letter from architect to contractor accepting claim

This letter is not suitable for use with MW 80

Dear Sir

[*insert appropriate heading*]

I refer to your claim for loss and/or expense, under clause 26[1] of the conditions, received on [*insert date*].

After careful consideration of the evidence, I am of the opinion that there is some merit in your claim and I am proceeding/I am asking the quantity surveyor [*omit as appropriate*] to ascertain the amount of such loss and/or expense. The amount so ascertained will be added to the next certificate after the ascertainment has been completed.

[*Add if appropriate:*]

In carrying out the ascertainment, regard will be made to the following extension(s) of the time made under clause 25:[2] [*insert the appropriate extensions of time and clause numbers*].

Yours faithfully

Copy: Quantity surveyor

---

[1]   *Substitute '4.11' when using IFC 84*
[2]   *Omit this paragraph when using IFC 84*

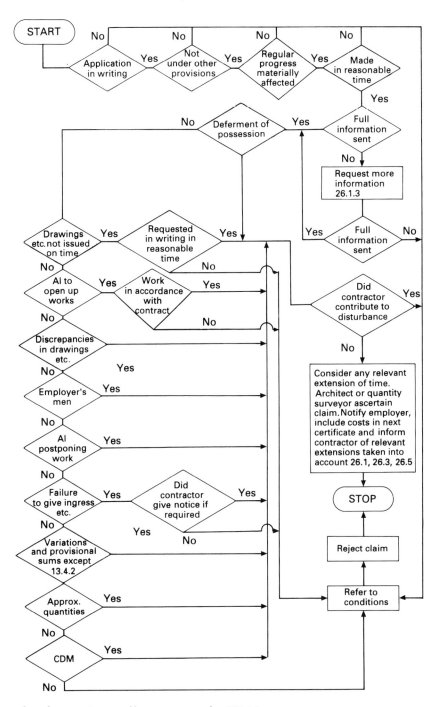

Flowchart 8 Loss and/or expense under JCT 80.

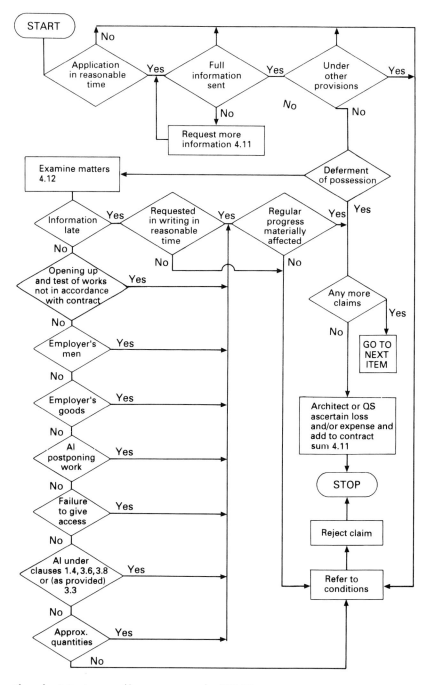

Flowchart 9 Loss and/or expense under IFC 84.

Basically, before ascertainment can take place, you have to decide on all the available evidence whether the regular progress of the works has been substantially affected by deferment of possession or by an occurrence which falls under one of the matters in clause 26.2. Then you must be sure that the contractor cannot recover reimbursement by the application of some other term of the contract. After that, either you, or more usually the quantity surveyor, will carry out the actual ascertainment.

Much has been written about the methods to be employed in deciding whether there is a claim or not. Clearly you may be faced with the protests of the contractor if you reject his claim. How you counter will depend upon the circumstances. Just remember that the grant of extension of time does not automatically entitle the contractor to loss and/or expense. The contractor's claim must be well founded to succeed. Many contractors try a claim almost as a matter of course. The quality of the substantiating evidence will usually indicate whether a claim is serious or not.

IFC 84

This section is generally applicable and the steps in considering a claim for loss and/or expense are set out in **Flowchart 9**. The applicable clauses are 4.11 and 4.12 which outline a simplified procedure to JCT 80.

MW 80

Amendment MW 5:1988 introduced into clause 3.6 a provision allowing you to include in any valuation of an instruction any direct loss and/or expense incurred by the contractor due to regular progress of the works being affected by compliance. This is a fairly limited entitlement not dependent on any application by the contractor although, in practice, doubtless he will make one. If the contractor incurs loss and/or expense due to any cause other than compliance with your instructions, you have no power to consider it. You must refer such claims to the employer. They are essentially common law claims and unless the employer is prepared to deal with them, the contractor must pursue them through the courts or in arbitration.

L Completion

L1 Defects liability period: urgent defects (132)

At any time between practical completion and before the expiry of the defects liability period, you are empowered, by clause 17.3 of the conditions, to issue instructions to the contractor to make good any defects which are his responsibility (see L5). No doubt you will only do this if the defects are of an urgent nature, but you can issue such instructions as often as you feel is necessary.

If you have cause to issue several such instructions during the defects liability period, the contractor may well protest that you are being unreasonable and that he is losing money. He may suggest that, whereas one such instruction may be justified, the remainder of the defects should wait until the expiry of the defects liability period. If you are satisfied that your instructions are 'necessary' for whatever reason, write to the contractor.

IFC 84

Clause 2.10 is in slightly different terms and gives you power to notify defects to the contractor not later than 14 days after the expiry of the defects liability period. The effect, however, is similar in that you can issue the instructions at any time during the period.

MW 80

The situation is unlikely to arise because the defects liability period is normally quite short and clause 2.5 is very brief, apparently giving you the power to require the defects to be made good as they arise during the period.

132   Letter from architect to contractor regarding urgent defects

This letter is only suitable for use with JCT 80

Dear Sir

[*insert appropriate heading*]

Thank you for your letter of [*insert date*].

Notwithstanding the provisions of clause 17.2 of the conditions, clause 17.3 empowers me to issue instructions regarding the making good of defects whenever I consider it necessary to do so.

All the instructions issued in respect of the making good of defects since practical completion was certified have been issued because I considered them necessary. It is not my wish to cause you needless work or expense and any items which can wait until the expiry of the defects liability period will be dealt with at that time.

I should be pleased if you would carry out my instructions of [*insert date*] forthwith, otherwise I shall be obliged to issue a notice requiring compliance with my instructions in accordance with clause 4.1.2.

Yours faithfully

L2 Defects liability period: issue of list (133), (instruction 4)

About a week before the end of the defects liability period you should inspect the works and make a list of all the defects which are apparent and which you consider are the contractor's responsibility. The list may be drawn up in the form of an architect's instruction and delivered to the contractor not later than 14 days after the expiration of the defects liability period. All well and good but there are numerous things which can go wrong.

What if you simply forgot to issue a list? Perhaps you drew up a list, sent it for typing and it failed to reappear. For whatever reason, let us imagine that the contractor does not receive your list within 14 days. What should you do? The first and most obvious action is to issue the list just as soon as you remember. Do it in a perfectly normal manner. There is a chance that the contractor will simply get on with the work (although you are technically in breach of your duty under the contract). The chance of this happening is increased if:

❑ Your list is only a week or so late
❑ The defects are relatively minor
❑ The contractor is anxious to please
❑ You have behaved in a reasonable manner throughout the contract period

If the contractor writes to inform you that he is under no obligation to attend to any defects which are notified more than 14 days after the end of the defects liability period, you can write him letter **133**.

The situation is that the contractor's obligation is to carry out and complete the work in accordance with the contract. If he fails to do this, he is in breach of contract as evidenced by defects appearing during the defects liability period and the contract allows him to return to site and put things right. If he does not wish to take advantage of this opportunity the employer is entitled to use his common law rights to recover the cost of rectifying the faults. In practice, deducting the cost from monies due avoids paying the money and having to sue for its return.

IFC 84

The position under this form is very much the same.

133 Letter from architect to contractor regarding late issue of schedule of defects

RECORDED DELIVERY

Dear Sir

[*insert appropriate heading*]

Thank you for your letter of [*insert date*].

I accept that the schedule of defects was delivered later than prescribed in the conditions.[1] However, the situation is that the defects amount to a breach of your contractual obligations. I cannot state that the defects are not present and, therefore, I cannot issue a certificate in accordance with clause 17.4.[2] Two important results are that no further release of retention can be made and, similarly,[3] I cannot issue a final certificate.

The employer is entitled to employ others to carry out the work and deduct the cost from any further payments due to you. If you do not inform me within seven days from the date of this letter that you will carry out the work immediately, I shall advise the employer accordingly.

Yours faithfully

Copy: Clerk of works

---

[1]   *Omit when using MW 80*
[2]   *Substitute '2.5' when using MW 80 or '2.10' when using IFC 84*
[3]   *Substitute 'therefore', when using MW 80*

Architect's instruction 4: Schedule of defects

Defects liability period – schedule of defects

Make good the following defects entirely at your own cost:

[*Insert the list of defects, but not the manner of making good.*]

Please inform me when all the defects have been made good.

Copies: Employer
Clerk of works

MW 80

Clause 2.5 makes provision for a defects liability period. There is no specific requirement for a schedule of defects and it seems that you can require defects to be made good at any time during the period. It would be good practice for you to issue a list, however, and provided that you are not excessively late in doing so, the contractor has little ground for complaint. Instruction 4 and letter **133** are applicable.

L3 Defects liability period: items overlooked (134)

If you issue the list on time and the contractor makes good but you find, on re-inspection, that you have overlooked some items, you are in a difficult situation. Clause 17.3 prevents you from issuing further instructions for the making good of defects appearing within the defects liability period after you have delivered a schedule of defects to the contractor. Such defects are, of course, breaches of contract and although you can no longer insist that the contractor rectifies them, the employer is certainly entitled to recover the cost of rectification from the contractor. It is likely, although by no means universally accepted, that you can still issue an instruction to open up the works under clause 8.3 or to remove from site work not in accordance with the contract under clause 8.4.

Depending upon the contractor, the best way might be to telephone him and explain the problem. If the defects are minor, one or two things might result:

❏ The contractor will agree to carry out the making good
❏ The contractor will agree to carry out the making good if the employer pays

If the defects are major, and a telephone call does not succeed, you could try a letter.

Strictly, of course, you cannot refuse to issue a certificate of making good defects if the original schedule of defects has been completed in all respects. The certificate of making good defects signals the release of the remaining retention, however. Similarly, the contract calls for the issue of the final certificate within the time specified in the appendix. It would be negligent to issue a certificate stating your satisfaction, however, if you are not so satisfied. If the contractor continues to refuse to make good defects, you may advise your client to

134 Letter from architect to contractor if defects omitted from schedule of defects

This letter is not suitable for use with MW 80

RECORDED DELIVERY

Dear Sir

[*insert appropriate heading*]

I refer to my telephone conversation of [*insert date*] with [*insert name*] and I regret that you feel unable to make good the defects I mentioned. The defects are:

[*Insert list of defects omitted from the schedule of defects.*]

The conditions of contract prevent me from instructing you to make good the defects. Nevertheless, the defects are breaches of contract on your part for which the employer has the right to claim damages. Such damages would be the cost of having the defects made good by others. Rather than take such a step, the employer is willing to allow you to return to site and make good provided you so notify me within seven days from the date of this letter.

Perhaps you would care to reconsider your decision so that matters can be brought to a satisfactory conclusion.

Yours faithfully

Copy: Quantity surveyor

have the defects made good by others and deduct the cost as damages from any monies payable to the contractor.

IFC 84

Although clause 2.10 does not specifically prohibit you from issuing further instructions, the general position must be very much the same as described under JCT 80.

MW 80

Because there is no specific provision to prevent you issuing instructions after a schedule of defects has been issued, it would appear that you can do so, provided that you have not issued a certificate of making good defects.

L4 Defects liability period: contractor slow in remedying defects (135)

Clause 17.2 requires the contractor to make good defects within a reasonable time after receipt of the schedule of defects. 'Reasonable' will mean different periods of time in the context of differing contracts. It is suggested that the contractor should normally make a start within two weeks of receiving the schedule. It may well be reasonable to expect all defects to be made good within a month, depending on their nature and extent. No precise guidance can be given. If you decide that the contractor is carrying out his work with unacceptable dilatoriness, you must tell him so.

IFC 84 and MW 80

Although there is no specific provision for the contractor to make good defects within a reasonable time, such a provision must be implied otherwise the contractor could take years over the process. Letter **135** is applicable.

If the contractor's work does not improve, you will have to carry out your threat (see K13).

135 Letter from architect to contractor if slow in making good defects

Dear Sir

[*insert appropriate heading*]

I draw your attention to my instruction number [*insert number*] dated [*insert date*] containing a schedule of defects.

It is my opinion that you are not complying with the provisions of the contract in that you are not[1] making good the defects within a reasonable time.

If your progress does not improve forthwith, you will oblige me to issue a notice requiring compliance with my instruction in accordance with clause 4.1.2.[2]

Yours faithfully

---

[1] *Omit when using IFC 84 or MW 80*
[2] *Substitute '3.5' when using IFC 84 or MW 80*

L5 Defects liability period: contractor claims some items are not defects (136)

The contractor may well dispute some items in your schedule of defects. Clause 17.2 states the contractor's responsibilities. Provided that the items are defects, shrinkages or other faults similar to defects and shrinkages and are due to either materials or workmanship not being in accordance with the contract, or frost occurring before the date certified for practical completion, he is liable to make them good.

It sounds straightforward but, in practice, it is all too easy to get involved in fruitless argument. Sit down and think about his points. If you decide that he is correct, concede the items with good grace. If you decide that he is wrong, make your decision equally clear.

IFC 84

Clause 2.10 deals with defects liability. The remarks in this section are generally applicable.

MW 80

Clause 2.5 makes similar provisions and the remarks in this section are generally applicable, as is letter **136**.

L6 Defects liability period: client's refusal to allow making good (137), (138), (139)

In certain circumstances the client may refuse to allow the contractor to make good defects in some areas which would cause considerable upheaval to the client's activities. This is perfectly understandable from the client's point of view. The contract provides that, with the employer's consent, you may instruct the contractor not to make good certain defects and make an appropriate deduction from the contract sum. You should not consider such action if the defects in question are other than merely cosmetic. If you consider the defect must be put right, you must write to the employer; do not simply telephone **(137)**. In the case of trivial defects the client must send you a waiver of his rights under the contract in very clear terms **(138)**. The employer may think that he is entitled to have deducted from the contract sum the cost of getting the defects remedied by others, although that would be more than it would cost the contractor to do the work. In that he is mistaken and you must tell him so in writing **(139)**.

136 Letter from architect to contractor if he incorrectly disputes items in the schedule of defects

Dear Sir

[*insert appropriate heading*]

Thank you for your letter of [*insert date*].

Having carefully considered the points you raise, I am satisfied that every item you mention is a defect, shrinkage[1] or other fault due to materials or workmanship not being in accordance with the contract or frost occurring before practical completion of the works.

Yours faithfully

---

[1] *Substitute 'excessive shrinkage' when using MW 80*

137 Letter from architect to client if he refuses to allow defects to be made good

Dear Sir

[insert appropriate heading]

I understand that you do not require the contractor to make good the following defects because his activities would seriously disrupt your operations:

[List the defects that the client does not require making good.]

Although the contract allows me to instruct the contractor not to make good provided that I have your consent, the defects in question are more than merely cosmetic and, if not rectified, the consequences will be serious. In the circumstances, I should not be carrying out my professional duties properly if I issued such an instruction.

The defects must be corrected. This is an important matter and I will visit you on [insert date] at [insert time] to discuss the implications in greater detail. Please let me know if that arrangement is not convenient.

Yours faithfully

138   Letter from architect to client requiring waiver

Dear Sir

[insert appropriate heading]

I understand that you do not require the contractor to make good the following defects because his activities would seriously disrupt your own operations:

[List the defects that the client does not require making good.]

The contract allows me to instruct the contractor not to make good provided I have your consent.

I should be pleased therefore if you would confirm the following:

1   You do not require the contractor to carry out any making good of the defects listed above.

2   You waive any rights you may have against any persons in regard to the items listed as defects in the above-mentioned list of defects and not made good.

3   You indemnify me against any expense, liability, loss, claim or proceedings whatsoever arising under any statute or at common law in respect of personal injury or death of any person and/or damage to any real or personal property arising out of, in connection with or as a result of any or all of the above listed defects not being made good.

Yours faithfully

139 Letter from architect to client if he wants to deduct cost of making good by others

Dear Sir

[*insert appropriate heading*]

Following our meeting/telephone conversation [*as appropriate*] on [*insert date*], it occurred to me that I may not have been as clear as I intended when explaining the 'appropriate deduction' for defects you have decided not to have made good.

On the basis that all defects are breaches of contract and that you are entitled to damages, you must try to mitigate your loss. The defects liability provisions are in the contract to give the contractor the opportunity to put defects right himself. That is obviously cheaper than getting another contractor to do the work. If you opt not to allow him to make good, the contract only allows you to have the benefit of the contractor's own costs. In other words, you cannot penalise him for your own decision.

If, on the other hand, you decide not to allow him to make good simply because his workmanship has been so poor that you have lost all confidence in him, you would be entitled to the cost of paying another contractor, but that is not the situation here.

I hope that helps to explain the position.

Yours faithfully

IFC 84

This section is applicable to this form of contract.

MW 80

This section is applicable although the provisions of 2.5 are not detailed.

L7 Final certificate: contractor demands issue (140)

For various reasons, the contractor may write demanding the issue of the final certificate, and you may not be ready to comply. Clause 30.8 stipulates that the final certificate shall be issued not later than two months dating from:

❑ The end of the defects liability period; *or*
❑ The completion of making good defects; *or*
❑ The date the architect sent the contractor a copy of the ascertainment and statement of adjustments to the contract sum,

whichever is the latest.

The end of the defects liability period appears to apply only when there is no schedule of defects – a very unusual situation. The completion of making good defects implies the issue of your certificate to that effect. The commonest reason for apparent delay is because the contractor is slow in providing the information in accordance with clause 30.6.1.1 for adjustment of the contract sum. You must make your position clear.

IFC 84

Clause 4.6 stipulates that the final certificate must be issued within 28 days of:

❑ The issue of a making good of defects certificate; *or*
❑ The sending of computations of the adjusted contract sum to the contractor,

whichever is the latest.

140 Letter from architect to contractor refusing to issue the final certificate

Dear Sir

[*insert appropriate heading*]

Thank you for your letter of [*insert date*].

I am unable to issue the final certificate because

[*Use the appropriate following phrase:*]

you have not yet completed the making good of defects in accordance with clause 17[1].

I have/the quantity surveyor has [*use appropriate expression*] not yet received all the necessary documentation in accordance with clause 30.6.1.1.[2] When you have fulfilled your obligations you will make it possible for the final certificate to be issued.

Yours faithfully

Copy: Quantity surveyor

---

[1]   *Substitute '2.10' when using IFC 84 and '2.5' when using MW 80*
[2]   *Substitute '4.5' when using IFC 84 and '4.4' when using MW 80*

MW 80

The contractor may write demanding issue of the final certificate and you may not be ready to comply. Clause 4.4 stipulates that the final certificate shall be issued within 28 days of the receipt of all the contractor's documentation reasonably required for the computation of the amount to be finally certified. The contractor must supply such documentation within three months (or such period as is noted in the conditions) of the date of practical completion; always provided that you have issued a certificate of making good defects.

The usual reason for delay in issuing the final certificate is lack of the necessary documents. Letter **140** is applicable.

L8 Client: overspending notification (Fig. 2)

This is the subject of many headaches. How to tell the client that his building has cost him more than he thought. It is linked to section 10.32. If you have kept your client informed, on a regular basis, the final account should not come as a shock and, given the in-built pessimism of most quantity surveyors during the progress of the works, it might be a nice surprise. You might have a problem if your client would not have embarked on the building project at all had he known the true cost at the beginning. This section assumes that the overspend does not fall into that category.

Psychology is all important. Your statement to the client showing the final account should be straightforward, clear and brief. Arrange the various items so that he can easily see the cause of the overspending. Above all, do not make the mistake of being apologetic about it. Unless you have made some gigantic mistake, he is getting what he paid for. Or, put another way, he is paying for what he has got. Most people are reasonable and, provided you do not lead him to think that you are trying to keep something from him, your client should have no complaints (Fig. 2).

IFC 84

This section is also applicable to this contract.

MW 80

This section is applicable, with the appropriate statement of final account, except for the reference to the quantity surveyor who will rarely be used on this type of contract.

For use with JCT 80 or IFC 84, statement as follows:

Contract sum	£
<u>Deduct</u> contingencies	£
<u>Add</u> sundry additional works (brief details)	£ _____
	£
<u>Deduct</u> (or <u>add</u>) adjustment of PC and provisional sums	£
<u>Deduct</u> (or <u>add</u>) adjustment of measured work	£ _____
	£
<u>Add</u> fluctuations	£ _____
	£
<u>Add</u> reimbursement of loss and/or expense under clause 26	£ _____
<u>Final amount</u>	£ _____

For use with MW 80, statement as follows:

Contract sum	£
<u>Deduct</u> contingencies	£
<u>Add</u> sundry additional works (brief details)	£ _____
	£
<u>Deduct</u> (or <u>add</u>) adjustment of provisional sums	£ _____
	£
<u>Add</u> fluctuations (if clause 4.5 operative)	£ _____
<u>Final amount</u>	£ _____

Fig. 2 Statement of final account to client.

L9 As-built records, if contractor or sub-contractor will not supply (141)

It is assumed that you have inserted a requirement in the contract documents that the contractor must supply 'as-built' records at the end of the job and that similar requirements have been inserted in the sub-contract specifications. Such records serve a very useful function in the future maintenance of the building, it being recognised that the finished building may differ from the original drawings in important and often invisible respects. It is particularly true of drainage, heating and electrical services.

The contractor should keep records of the work as it progresses. The preparation of 'as-built' records at the end of a job is a tedious pro-

141   Letter from architect to contractor requiring 'as-built' records

Dear Sir

[*insert appropriate heading*]

Thank you for your letter of [*insert date*].

I recognise that the preparation of 'as-built' records is a tedious procedure. However, these records are vital for the proper maintenance of the building and they are clearly required in the contract documents.

[*Indicate position in documents by reference to bills of quantities or specification and page numbers.*]

You are deemed to have included for them in the overall tender figure and I must insist that you provide them. Depending on the quality of your own records, this may involve you in contacting the appropriate sub-contractors.

Please inform me, during the next week, of the date on which I can expect to receive a full set of the drawings. It need hardly be stated, I trust, that you must bear full responsibility for the completeness and accuracy of such drawings.

Yours faithfully

cedure which the contractor may try to avoid, even though he should have included the cost in his price. If he makes objection you must spell it out to him.

L10 Drawings: contractor fails to return them after job completed (142)

Many architects do not bother to request the return of drawings, schedules, etc. at the end of the contract. Clause 5.6 of the conditions requires the contractor to return them after final payment if you do request them. If he fails to comply, it is as well to inform him of your rights, for record purposes, although it is probably not worth going to great lengths to retrieve the drawings unless you have a particular reason.

IFC 84 and MW 80

There is no provision for the contractor to return your drawings, schedules, etc. at the end of the job. You can, of course, insert such a provision in the specification. In any case, there is no reason why you should not request their return. If he fails to comply, letter **142** is applicable.

L11 Defects after final certificate: latent defects (143), (144)

Defects which become apparent after the final certificate has been issued will probably be referred to you by the employer in the first instance. If your client actually accuses you of, or implies, negligence, consult your solicitor and inform your insurers. If he is simply notifying you and asking for help, go and have a look. Your inspection might indicate a latent defect on the part of the contractor.

It is obviously in your interests to be involved from the outset in any investigation and rectification of defects, but do not fall into the trap of doing large amounts of additional work without payment **(143)**. Assuming your client wishes you to deal with the matter for him and he will pay your fees, write to the contractor **(144)**.

The contractor will usually agree to inspect but he may disclaim responsibility. You must explain to him that, if he does not carry out remedial work, your client will take action at common law to obtain redress. Of course, you may simply get a solicitor's letter in reply to

142 Letter from architect to contractor if he fails to return drawings on request

Dear Sir

[*insert appropriate heading*]

I refer to my letter of [*insert date*] requesting return of all drawings, schedules and other like documents bearing my name which have been issued in connection with the above contract.

Since you have not complied with my request I draw your attention to clause 5.6 of the conditions which specifically provides for their return.[1]

The documents are my copyright and neither they nor the information contained therein may be used for any purpose whatsoever without my express written permission.

Yours faithfully

Copies: Employer
Consultants (including quantity surveyor)
Clerk of works

---

[1] *Omit underlined paragraph when using IFC 84 or MW 80*

143 Letter from architect to client regarding latent defects

Dear Sir

[*insert appropriate heading*]

Thank you for your letter of [*insert date*].

I inspected the [*specify what you inspected*] today and, at first sight, my opinion is [*insert your initial conclusions*].

The original contractor should be involved. I shall be happy to deal with the matter for you if you wish and a copy of the RIBA *Standard Form of Agreement for the Appointment of an Architect* (SFA 92) is enclosed, together with details of fees and expenses, for your information.

Yours faithfully

144   Letter from architect to contractor regarding latent defects

Dear Sir

[*insert appropriate heading*]

My client asked me to inspect a defect in the above works which became apparent on or about [*insert the date as near as possible*].

Having carried out a preliminary inspection, my opinion is that the defect is your responsibility. I should be pleased if you would telephone me as soon as possible to arrange a joint inspection.

Yours faithfully

your letter to the contractor. If so or if he just refuses to do the remedial work, advise your client to obtain specialist legal advice, arrange it for him and be present when it is given. The implications of defects at this stage are so complex that you should carefully consider the following points:

- ❏ You issued the final certificate and it is conclusive evidence that where you have particularly called for the quality of workmanship or materials to be to your satisfaction whether by reference on drawings or in the bills of quantities, they are to your satisfaction. This is not the same as certifying that the works are in every way correct. Indeed, it simply means that things which you have reserved for your approval in the contract documents are approved. It could be significant, however, if you have reserved for your approval the very thing which now proves defective.
- ❏ Is the defect such as you ought to have noticed during your inspections of the work?
- ❏ Could the defect be attributed to a design deficiency? If so, is it your design or that of the contractor, nominated sub-contractor or supplier? The contractor has limited design responsibility to the employer under this form of contract, and then only if the provisions for performance specified work or the contractor's designed portion supplement are used. If he has, in fact, carried out the design of the defective item, it may be because you failed to do so. Such a situation commonly occurs when an architect does not completely detail something and the contractor, trying to make progress, thinks he knows what is required and presses on. It may be that, in certain specific instances, the contractor assumes a design responsibility in such circumstances, but in general you owe the employer a duty to design the works and the duty is one which you cannot delegate to someone else without the employer's express authority. The situation with nominated sub-contractors or suppliers is that they owe no design duty to the contractor, but they can be put in contractual relationship with the employer by the completion of collateral warranties. It is essential to do so and also to obtain the employer's authority to delegate any design responsibility. A latent defect which seems to stem from a shortcoming in the nominated sub-contractor's design can be pursued by the employer directly against the nominated sub-contractor by virtue of the collateral warranty (NSC/W for nominated sub-contractors, TNS/2 for nominated suppliers).

If you are in doubt, you should get expert advice regarding any liabilities you might have and the best way to deal with them.

IFC 84

In general, the remarks in this section also apply to this form of contract. There is no provision for giving the contractor any formal design responsibility. There are no nominated sub-contractors or suppliers, but there are named persons as sub-contractors and the appropriate warranty form is ESA/1.

MW 80

The remarks in this section under IFC 84 are generally applicable, but it should be noted that the final certificate is not conclusive at all and there is no provision for nominated sub-contractors or suppliers nor collateral warranties.

M Feedback

M1 Complaints from client (145)

Feedback from completed jobs is an important method of checking procedures and the performance of the finished building in use. Many architects send a questionnaire to their clients at this stage. Some architects consider this is inviting trouble. Much, of course, will depend upon the particular client and his attitude to life. Generally your client, particularly if you carry out regular commissions for him, will be very pleased that you care about your work and he will recognise that your motive is to improve your service.

Occasionally, however, the feedback comes in the form of a complaint. If latent defects are indicated, you should proceed as in L11. If the complaints are of a more general nature, perhaps related to the working of the building rather than a constructional problem, you should write a friendly letter and follow it with a personal visit. Then you can discuss the precise nature of his complaint which probably arises from a variation in the way he uses it now that he is in occupation.

145 Letter from architect to client if complaining about the building use

Dear Sir

[*insert appropriate heading*]

Thank you for your letter of [*insert date*].

I always endeavour to carry out a feedback exercise after a project has been completed. I have found it useful for ironing out any problems that may arise after the building has been in use for a period.

I am grateful for your response, which is most interesting, and suggest that I should call and see you within the next few days to discuss the various points you raise. I shall be free [*indicate free dates*] and I should be grateful if you would telephone and let me know which date is most convenient for you.

Yours faithfully

Appendix 1

How to write letters

1.01 Introduction

Much of the architect's time is spent writing letters. It is surprising that very little guidance is given on this difficult subject during the average architectural course. It is usually left for the newly qualified architect to pick up the art of letter writing as he progresses through various offices.

Clearly, no amount of teaching and practice in schools could create the real conditions found in practice with their endless diversity. The possible exception might be the teaching office. Practice makes perfect and there is no substitute for experience, but some form of guidance may be useful and what follows can be considered useful hints.

1.02 What to say and how to say it effectively in writing

Before you write any letter ask yourself:

- ❏ Is the letter really necessary?
- ❏ What do I want to say exactly?

The sort of letter it is always necessary to write includes:

- ❏ Confirming oral conversations
- ❏ Answering questions
- ❏ Giving information
- ❏ Requesting information

Most letters fall into one or other of these categories and sometimes embrace several at once.

One of the commonest faults is to begin to write a letter without clearly knowing what you are going to say. Dictation is a difficult art to master for this reason.

Unless your letter is a 'one-liner', always make notes. Ensure that your notes cover all the points and then put them in the order in which you wish to include them in your letter. Usually, if it is a long letter, put generalities at the beginning or the end (but not both) and reserve the bulk of the letter for specifics. If practicable, it is a good idea to number the items so that the recipient can simply refer to the numbers when answering. Some very long letters are better written as a short report.

Keep your sentences short. Re-read your draft to make sure that you have made yourself absolutely clear. Communication is a difficult art. Avoid seeming apologetic if you have nothing for which to apologise. Phrases such as 'I regret' may be acceptable in some circumstances but avoid 'I am sorry to say'. The difference may seem slight but it is there nonetheless.

Architects are often accused of arrogance. The accusers, needless to say, are generally contractors. There is, however, a measure of truth in the accusation in that an architect may often seem arrogant if his letters are viewed through the eyes of a contractor. Try not to fall into that trap. Remember that one day your letters may be evidence before an arbitrator. The issue may turn on whether you have acted reasonably in making a decision. Reasonable decisions are made by reasonable men who, in turn, write reasonable letters. If your letters appear arrogant to a third party, are you likely to be thought capable of making a reasonable decision? Similarly, do not give vent to annoyance. Be totally reasonable even if unyielding in your point of view. The fictitious exchange in letters **146** and **147** illustrates the point.

1.03 Answering letters: the art of isolating the main points

You will sometimes receive letters which are quite simply a confused mess. How are they to be answered?

The first thing to do is to decide why the letters are so confused. Is it because the person writing lacks the basic skills to express himself clearly or is it a deliberate attempt to confuse the issues? Your own knowledge of the person concerned will be a major factor in your conclusions. If in doubt, it is always safer to assume a deliberate attempt at confusion. One way to answer such letters is for you, in effect, to rewrite the letter in the way you think it was intended and then answer that. Be careful, however, because you may be doing just what your correspondent wants – asking your own questions and answering them. You may say more than is necessary.

A safer way is first of all to list the points you have to answer; no matter that they are confused in the letter. For example, if the letter refers to extensions of time coupled with breaches of contract and the site agent's impending holiday, all in one muddled sentence, your letter

146   Letter from contractor to architect

Dear Sir

[*insert appropriate heading*]

I have received your letter of [*insert date*] and view the contents with disgust.

Seldom has my company had to deal with an architect who conducts his affairs in so high-handed, I may almost say, arrogant, a manner.

I have always strived for a good working relationship but it would seem that you do not share that view.

If you do not reconsider your decision, arbitration is the next step.

Yours faithfully

147   Letter from architect to contractor

Dear Sir

[*insert appropriate heading*]

Thank you for your letter of [*insert date*].

I regret that you do not agree with the decision expressed in my earlier letter of [*insert date*]. It was reached after careful consideration and I can see no grounds for altering it. Any further representations you care to make on any point in connection with the contract will receive my careful attention provided that they are accompanied by appropriate substantiation.

I sincerely trust that the good working relationship achieved on this contract will endure for the benefit of all parties.

Yours faithfully

should treat them one at a time, briefly. Devote one sentence to each and avoid linking events together yourself unless your correspondent has done so in a very clear way.

Another method of getting at the nub of the letter is to identify and answer just one point from the letter but be careful to state that the remainder of the letter 'is not understood'.

It may be a painstaking business, but over a series of exchanges you should be able gradually to sort out precisely what the other party is saying.

1.04 Obscurities: on both sides

There will be occasions when you do not understand at all what your correspondent is trying to say. Do not be afraid to write back and say precisely that. If he is honest in his approach, he will rephrase his letter. If he simply replies to the effect that he considers his previous letter perfectly clear, then he is obviously trying to make some capital out of it. All you have to do is to maintain your position and, if he wishes to make progress, he will be obliged to clarify himself sooner or later.

It is best to avoid obscurity in your own letters. Although some people do write, as a matter of policy almost, so that their letters can be read in two completely different ways, it is wise to strive for clarity. Deviously obscure letters can rebound on the writer. In this connection, always read other people's letters carefully. They may not actually mean what they appear to say at first glance.

1.05 Points to bear in mind

- ❑ It is always a good idea to write your letters thinking that, one day, they will be read out in court.
- ❑ If you simply acknowledge receipt of a letter you may be implying that you agree with its contents. If you are really pressed for time, acknowledge with the comment that you are considering the contents and will reply fully at a later date.
- ❑ In general, your correspondent can assume nothing if you do not reply. Phrases such as: 'If I do not hear from you by... you will be deemed to have agreed to my proposal' are meaningless. Sometimes it is wisest to stay silent. An exception is if the contract expressly gives silence a meaning. An example is JCT 80, clause 4.3.2, where, if you do not dissent from the contractor's confirmation of an oral instruction, the instruction takes effect.
- ❑ Leave yourself room to manoeuvre in later correspondence.
- ❑ Try to put yourself in the position of the person who will receive your letter.

❏ Always try to give your correspondent a dignified way out of a difficulty.

❏ If a correspondent is really causing you trouble, make a practice of answering all his letters with very short replies – one line if you can manage it.

❏ Pay attention to the arrangement of your letter. Bad news is usually better placed between two sections of good news. This is so that the recipient, in re-reading your letter, is always in the position of having to read some good news with the bad.

❏ Avoid business letter shorthand, e.g. 'ult.', 'inst.'.

❏ If writing about a contractual matter, you should use the actual words of the contract to make it clear that you are acting in accordance with the contract or giving some notice or certificate with contractual effect.

❏ Always strive to be honest and direct and confirm exactly what you said orally. It will earn you a good reputation.

A final point: communication is best achieved face to face. The next best thing is the telephone. Worst of all is the letter because it can give rise to misunderstandings which cannot be immediately corrected. However, letters are vital as a record of what each party intended at a particular time.

Read the letters in this book critically, bearing these points in mind. They are not carved in stone – merely a guide.

Appendix 2

How to make a decision

2.01 The problem

This section is intended to express in simple terms how decisions are made. **Flowchart 10** acts as a summary. You may think this is all nonsense, because you know, or have known, people who can make very quick and correct decisions and they do not go through this process. The truth is that some people can make very rapid and accurate decisions, because they instinctively know the process and they take all the factors into account extremely quickly. Such people are seldom aware that they are going through a process because it is a natural talent. You and I (certainly I) find making decisions difficult because our minds to not naturally operate in that way. It is, however, a skill which can be acquired.

Every decision you make is the response to a problem. Most decisions in building, particularly small decisions, are interwoven with other decisions. It is important to focus on them one at a time.

The first thing to clarify is whether the decision you have to make is major or minor, so that you can see how much time needs to be given to it. It is fruitless wasting hours on a decision which has very little implication, even if it is wrong. In order to determine the importance of a decision, you will have to do a little initial analysing. After you have ascertained the importance of the decision you have to make, you can proceed. In the case of major or minor decisions the method is the same; the expenditure of time is different.

Be absolutely clear what really is the problem. It may take some investigation. If the problem is major, write it down carefully. The act of writing something down, in itself, concentrates the mind on essentials. Rewrite your definition of the problem until you are absolutely certain that you have put everything down in the least number of words.

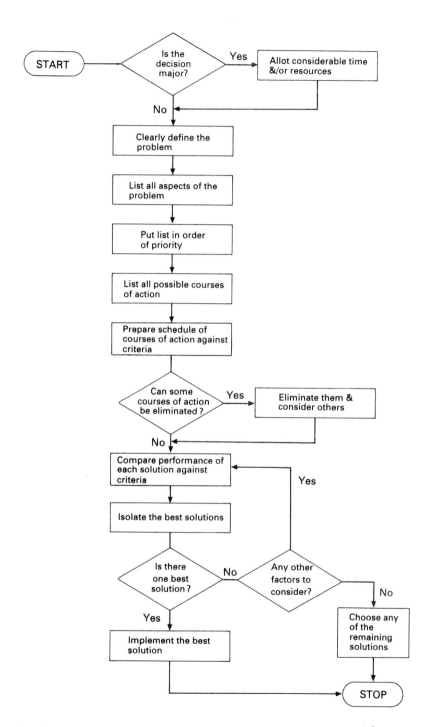

Flowchart 10 Making a decision.

2.02 *Getting things in order*

After the problem has been determined, you must examine all aspects of it. Some people adopt the practice of making a careful written appreciation of every item. Consider all the implications. Put down as many different points as you can, e.g. side-effects, financial or otherwise, opportunities, time scale, special conditions, physical or otherwise. This is best done in note form. Your first list will not have any particular sequence. Jot the points down as they come into your head. The next stage is to do some research to establish any other factors you should take into consideration. Your research will be with colleagues, on site, drawings, bills of quantities, specifications and any other publications which might have a bearing on the problem. By now your list may be pretty extensive.

The next step is to go through your list crossing out duplications and combining items which are closely linked. Prepare a new list by going through your rough draft and identifying the most important consideration and putting it at the top. Carry on this process until all the items are written down in order of importance. You have now assembled all the criteria for your decision and put them in order.

2.03 *Alternatives*

Take another sheet of paper. This time using the points from sheet 1, note the different possible ways of solving your problem. This is where some ingenuity or lateral thinking is useful to increase the number of possible solutions even if, at first sight, some of them may seem unlikely. At this stage you are probably uncertain whether some of the solutions will work. When you are as certain as you can be that you have covered all possible approaches to the problem, examine each one in turn against the criteria on sheet 1. Some of the solutions will work better than others in different areas. Make a schedule showing the good and bad results against your list of criteria. Some proposed solutions will be eliminated immediately.

2.04 *The decision*

You now have a sheet showing all the aspects of the problem in order of priority and another sheet listing possible solutions with a rating against each aspect. In some organisations the system has been developed to the point where you actually give numerical values to the ratings and use a complicated method of calculating the best solution. In the context of normal architectural practice such sophisticated techniques are usually unnecessary.

After eliminating the very poor solutions, you will generally have two or three possibles at the most. The decision is then made by comparing the way the solutions satisfy your criteria. In the event that two solutions appear equally satisfactory, for all points of view, you can either re-examine them to see if one is slightly better in some respect which you have hitherto not considered, or you must face the fact that you have two equally good solutions and choose either one.

2.05 When in doubt

There is an old saying: 'When in doubt – do nowt'. Like most old sayings, it contains a grain of truth. It means that if a problem arises which requires your decision and the solution is not immediately obvious, postpone your decision until you have gone through the analytical process described.

At the end of the process, you may find that there is nothing you can do to solve the problem adequately. That is rare. More usually, no solution solves the problem as adequately as you would wish. There are two things you can do. Find another solution or pick the best solution you have.

Of course, you do not have to cover your desk with sheets of paper for every decision you make. In many cases it will be enough to go through the stages in your mind.

The lack of ability to make a decision is really the lack of organised thinking. The mind revolves with a series of ideas, possibilities and fears. The simple exercise outlined in this section should enable you to get your thoughts in order. You may even acquire a reputation for decision-making! At the end of the process you can ask yourself two questions to help your decision:

❏ What is the worst thing that could happen if my particular decision is wrong?
❏ What should I *not* do?

Index